DIFFERENT
BY DESIGN

D0402245

DIFFERENT
BY DESIGN

JOHN MacARTHUR, JR.

While this book is intended for the reader's personal enjoyment and profit, it is also designed for study. A personal and group study guide is included at the end of this text.

East Parkway Church
Library
4700 East Roseville Parkway
Granite Bay, CA 95746

VICTOR BOOKS

A DIVISION OF SCRIPTURE PRESS PUBLICATIONS INC.
USA CANADA ENGLAND

Unless otherwise indicated, all Scripture references are from the *New American Standard Bible,* © the Lockman Foundation 1960, 1962, 1963, 1968, 1971, 1972, 1973, 1975, 1977; other references are from the *Holy Bible, New International Version®* (NIV). Copyright © 1973, 1978, 1984 by International Bible Society. Used by permission of Zondervan Publishing House. All rights reserved.

Copy Editor: Barbara Williams
Cover Design: Joe DeLeon
Recommended Dewey Decimal Classification: 248.84
Suggested Subject Heading: Christian Living
ISBN: 1-56676-247-5

© 1994 by John MacArthur, Jr. All rights reserved. Printed in the United States of America.

1 2 3 4 5 6 7 8 9 10   Printing/Year   98 97 96 95 94

No part of this book may be reproduced without written permission, except for brief quotations in books and critical reviews. For information, write Victor Books, 1825 College Avenue, Wheaton, Illinois 60187.

CONTENTS

INTRODUCTION

The fact that men and women are different by design is no surprise to those who are committed to reality or familiar with the Bible. It *is* a great surprise, however, to many who, over several decades, have engineered, vigorously endorsed, or passively succumbed to the social experiments that deny or attempt to alter that design. The experiments have failed, and have destroyed our culture in the process. A plethora of astute, honest, and brave observers in this closing decade of our century have begun to speak up:

• **Item:** In the former Soviet Union, where radical social experimentation on male/female roles has occurred since the early part of this century, "many Russian women see true freedom as the ability to be full-time wives and mothers," according to a front-page story in a recent issue of the *Los Angeles Times* (Elizabeth Shogren, "Russia's Equality Erosion" [Thur. 11 Feb. 1993], A1). That traditional option has long been denied them, and both men and women are beginning to sense that this denial was never right:

> Public opinion polls show that many Russians, men and women, feel that if they could have the choice, most women would not work outside the home while raising their children. . . .
>
> Lyudmila is one girl who has already decided that she does not want to repeat the double-duty life of her mother, who has toiled full time for 20 years in a candy factory while, like many other Russian women, being solely responsible for the household. "She gets no satisfaction from her work," said Lyudmila. . . . "I don't want to work after I am married. It takes too much time from your family. Most of my girlfriends feel the same way. . . ." "The majority of younger women think it's better if women are at home," said Valentina V. Bodrova, a sociologist at the All Russian Center of Public Opinion and Market Research, a leading polling organization (A10).

● **Item:** The cover of the January 20, 1992 issue of *Time* magazine reads, "Why Are Men and Women Different? It isn't just upbringing. New studies show they are born that way" (January 20, 1992). That title has the aura of a shocking revelation, but it really is common sense to objective people — as demonstrated by the opening illustration of the lead article:

Many scientists rely on elaborately complex and costly equipment to probe the mysteries confronting humankind. Not Melissa Hines. The UCLA behavioral scientist is hoping to solve one of life's oldest riddles with a toybox full of police cars, Lincoln Logs, and Barbie dolls. . . . Hines and her colleagues have tried to determine the origins of gender differences by capturing on videotape the squeals of delight, furrows of concentration and myriad decisions that children from 2 1/2 to 8 make while playing. Although both sexes play with all the toys available in Hines' laboratory, *her work confirms what most parents (and more than a few aunts, uncles and nursery-school teachers) already know.* As a group, the boys favor sports cars, fire trucks, and Lincoln Logs, while the girls are drawn more often to dolls and kitchen toys. . . .

During the feminist revolution of the 1970s, talk of inborn differences in the behavior of men and women was distinctly unfashionable, even taboo. . . . Once sexism was abolished, so the argument ran, the world would become a perfectly equitable, androgynous place, aside from a few anatomical details. But biology has a funny way of confounding expectations. Rather than disappear, the evidence for innate sexual differences only began to mount. . . .

Another generation of parents discovered that, despite their best efforts to give baseballs to their daughters and sewing kits to their sons, girls still flocked to dollhouses while boys clambered into tree forts (Christine Gorman, "Sizing Up the Sexes," p. 42, emphasis added).

8

• **Item:** A recent book on brain physiology, provocatively titled, *Brain Sex: The Real Difference Between Men and Women* (Anne Moir and David Jessel [New York: Dell, 1991]) details the empirical evidence for innate differences between the sexes. Anne Moir acquired her interest in the topic as a postgraduate student working for her doctorate in genetics at Oxford University amid the radical feminist atmosphere of the '70s. She noticed that some scientists seemed afraid of their discoveries about male/female differences, downplaying their significance over concern about what was politically correct. But Dr. Moir followed the mounting evidence through the years, and shared her findings with a reporter. The book that emerged from their joint effort has this significant introduction:

> Men are different from women. They are equal only in their common membership of the same species, humankind. To maintain that they are the same in aptitude, skill or behaviour is to build a society based on a biological and scientific lie.
>
> The sexes are different because their brains are different. The brain, the chief administrative and emotional organ of life, is differently constructed in men and in women; it processes information in a different way, which results in different perceptions, priorities and behaviour.
>
> In the past ten years there has been an explosion of scientific research into what makes the sexes different. Doctors, scientists, psychologists and sociologists, working apart, have produced a body of findings which, taken together, paints a remarkably consistent picture. And the picture is one of startling sexual asymmetry....
>
> It is time to explode the social myth that men and women are virtually interchangeable, all things being equal. All things are not equal (p. 5).

• **Item:** Another popular book on this general topic, which spent over two years on the *New York Times* bestseller list, is *You Just Don't Understand: Women and Men in*

Conversation by Dr. Deborah Tannen (New York: Ballantine, 1991). A previous book Tannen wrote had just one chapter out of ten on gender differences, but 90 percent of the requests she received for interviews, articles, and lectures were from people wanting to know more about male/female differences. She decided she also wanted to learn more. Tannen writes:

> I am joining the growing dialogue on gender and language because the risk of ignoring differences is greater than the danger of naming them. Sweeping something big under the rug doesn't make it go away; it trips you up and sends you sprawling. . . .
>
> Pretending that women and men are the same hurts women, because the ways they are treated are based on the norms for men. It also hurts men who, with good intentions, speak to women as they would to men, and are nonplussed when their words don't work as they expected, or even spark resentment and anger. . . . If we recognize and understand the differences between us, we can take them into account, adjust to, and learn from each other's styles (pp. 16–17).

● **Item:** One young single mother wrote a book asserting that the feminist movement has, first of all, failed women and children—with men not far behind. She points out that

> riffling through the pages of your daughters' [public] school books, what you won't see . . . is a single image celebrating the work women do as wives and mothers. That information . . . is carefully and systematically expunged from the official cultural record. Sexual equality is our culture's rationale for denying the existence of specifically female contributions, an excuse for withdrawing social approval and protection when women refuse to behave just like men. . . . When a culture begins to promote false conceptions of sex, gender, and family, the reverberations are felt immediately, penetrating deep into the least public and most intimate

realms of our daily lives (Maggie Gallagher, *Enemies of Eros* [Chicago: Bonus, 1989], 9, 21).

A recent article in *The Atlantic Monthly* described those reverberations in chilling detail. Its conclusion? That "over the past two and a half decades Americans have been conducting what is tantamount to a vast natural experiment in family life. . . . This is the first generation in the nation's history to do worse psychologically, socially, and economically than its parents" (Barbara Dafoe Whitehead, "Dan Quayle Was Right" [April 1993]:84).

● **Item:** During our nation's 1992 Presidential election, we received a moving reminder that many sensible people resisted the family experiments being foisted on society. Marilyn Quayle, wife of the former Vice President, said in a featured speech:

> Not everyone believed that the family was so oppressive that women could only thrive apart from it. . . . I sometimes think . . . liberals are . . . angry because they believed the grandiose promises of the liberation movements.
>
> They're disappointed because most women do not wish to be liberated from their essential natures as women. Most of us love being mothers and wives, which gives our lives a richness that few men or women get from professional accomplishment alone. . . . Nor has it made for a better society to liberate men from their obligations as husbands and fathers (Wed. 19 Aug. 1992, Republican National Convention, Houston, Texas, Transcript ID: 861194).

Christians all along have objected to intentional or unintentional obscuring of gender distinctives, writing many books of their own on the topic—and long before it became popular to do so. Some of those books focus exclusively on women and feminism; others discuss what the Bible teaches about both men and women, going into great detail about what life was like in ancient times, but falling a little short in providing guidelines on how that applies to contemporary life.

The approach of this book is not to provide you with an intimidating tome, but to explain simply and directly all the key biblical passages describing what it means to be a man or a woman from God's perspective. I want you to have a comprehensive picture, but not one that is overwhelming. I will also endeavor to be practical so you know how God's Word applies to your particular situation.

At the same time, you need to be aware of current trends threatening the clear biblical instruction on male/female roles. As is often the case, the church eventually catches the world's diseases and adopts the spirit of the age. Some leaders and writers, in the name of Christianity, teach principles that attempt to redefine, or even alter, biblical truths to accommodate the standards of contemporary thinking. When appropriate, we'll examine what they are teaching.

Part one will examine the various attacks against God's design for men and women, beginning with Satan's initial corruption of God's glorious creation and including some of the more contemporary assaults on specific biblical doctrines, like the principle of authority and submission. In part two we'll review God's design for marriage, particularly how life in Christ and being filled with His Spirit can bring fulfillment to any marriage. We'll also consider the specific problems wives face in a society that elevates self-fulfillment above family responsibility. I've also included one chapter for those of you who are either married to unbelievers, widowed, divorced, or single. Finally, part three examines God's design for the roles of men and women in the church, including the specific biblical qualifications for leading or serving.

To narrow our scope, one area of male/female interaction we won't consider in depth is family life, a topic I have covered extensively in other books (*The Fulfilled Family* and *The Family*, both published by Moody Press [Chicago: 1987, 1982]). Pushing past the failed social experiments we will endeavor to rediscover what God's timeless Word says about our differences as men and women, and the grand design and fulfillment that await those who embrace the truth.

PART ONE

The Attack
on God's Design

CHAPTER 1
Creation to Corruption

As our country prepared to enter a new decade, the cover of the December 4, 1989 issue of *Time* magazine declared, "Women Face the '90s: In the '80s they tried to have it all. Now they've just plain had it. Is there a future for feminism?" In the cover article the author, Claudia Wallis, asked, "Is the feminist movement—one of the great social revolutions of contemporary history—truly dead? Or is it merely stalled and in need of a little consciousness raising?" (p. 81) Wallis claims it isn't dead, just in transition.

Faced with a myriad of setbacks in the 1980s, including the defeat of the equal rights amendment, the more radical elements of the women's movement lost their voice and others were forced to moderate their position. Even Betty Friedan, the movement's leading advocate, was pressured to declare herself in favor of the nuclear family.

While the extremists of the movement and their more outlandish positions—such as the abolition of marriage and the

exaltation of lesbianism — no longer command the attention
they once did; the damage to our society has been done.
George Gilder, author of *Men and Marriage* (Gretna, La.:
Pelican, 1986) writes,

> Though rejecting feminist politics and lesbian posturing,
> American culture has absorbed the underlying ideology
> like a sponge. The principle tenets of sexual liberation
> or sexual liberalism — the obsolescence of masculinity
> and femininity, of sex roles, and of heterosexual monog-
> amy as the moral norm — have diffused through the sys-
> tem and become part of America's conventional wisdom.
>
> Taught in most of the nation's schools and colleges and
> proclaimed insistently in the media, sexual liberalism
> prevails even where feminism — at least in its antimale
> rhetoric — seems increasingly irrelevant (p. viii).

Unfortunately, the church is in the process of soaking up
some of the same ideology. More and more undiscerning
believers are falling prey to the feminist agenda. I am amazed
at how many evangelical churches, schools, and even seminaries are jettisoning doctrines they once defended as biblical
truths. Within evangelical Christianity there is an organiza-
tional counterpart to the feminist movement called Christians
for Biblical Equality that opposes any unique leadership role
for men in the family and the church. John Piper and Wayne
Grudem, in the introduction of *Recovering Biblical Manhood
and Womanhood* (Wheaton, Ill.: Crossway, 1991), describe the
supporters of this organization:

> These authors differ from secular feminists because
> they do not reject the Bible's authority or truthfulness,
> but rather give new interpretations of the Bible to sup-
> port their claims. We may call them "evangelical femi-
> nists" because by personal commitment to Jesus Christ
> and by profession of belief in the total truthfulness of
> Scripture they still identify themselves very clearly with
> evangelicalism. Their arguments have been detailed,
> earnest, and persuasive to many Christians.

What has been the result? Great uncertainty among evangelicals. Men and women simply are not sure what their roles should be. . . .

The controversy shows signs of intensifying, not sub-siding. Before the struggle ends, probably no Christian family and no evangelical church will remain untouched (p. xiii).

While many in our culture are attempting to remove femi-nist ideals from the mainstream of society, the church has allowed access to those same ideals within her hallowed walls. But we shouldn't be surprised, because the feminist attack on the people of God is as old as man. Feminism began in the Garden when Eve, who we could call the first feminist, listened to Satan's lies, stepped out from under Adam's au-thority, acted independently, and led the human race into sin.

Satan's goal from the start has been to overthrow God's design for His elect. That's why it's so tragic when the church is duped into helping him carry out his assault on God. What ought to be the strongest bastion of the truth of God is falling fast to the march of the feminist army. Those of us who hold to the integrity of God's Word cannot let it fall victim to the warped society around us.

Scripture is very clear about the place God has designed for men and women in society, in the family, and in the church. And it is to Scripture we must turn to reaffirm the wonders of God's design.

GOD'S PERFECT DESIGN

Any examination of the role of men and women in God's design must begin with an understanding of Genesis 1–3. The key verses in those chapters provide a foundation for the texts we will examine in future chapters.

God's Image-bearers as Co-regents

Genesis 1:27-28 gives the account of the creation of man and woman:

God created man in His own image, in the image of God

He created him; male and female He created them. And
God blessed them; and God said to them, "Be fruitful
and multiply, and fill the earth, and subdue it; and rule
over the fish of the sea and over the birds of the sky,
and over every living thing that moves on the earth."

Notice two important things in that account. First, God
created *both* man and woman in His image. Not just man, but
woman also was made in God's image. Like God, each has a
rational personality. Men and women alike possess intellect,
emotion, and will, by which they are able to think, feel, and
choose. Humanity was not, however, created in God's image
as perfectly holy and unable to sin. Nor were man and woman
created in His image essentially. They have never possessed
His supernatural attributes, such as omniscience, omnipo-
tence, immutability, or omnipresence. People are only human, not at all divine.

Author J. David Pawson reminds us that the male-female
equality of creation in God's image also "does not mean inter-
changeability. A cylinder head and a crankcase may be of the
same material, size, weight, and cost—but they cannot be
exchanged" *(Leadership Is Male* [Nashville: Thomas Nelson,
1990], 25).

Second, God blessed them as man and woman in verse 28:
"God said to *them,* 'Be fruitful and multiply . . . fill the
earth . . . subdue it; and rule' " (emphasis added). The man
and woman were co-regents: God gave both Adam and Eve
the task to rule *together* over the lower creation.

The Perfect Relationship
Genesis 2:7 describes the creation of man in greater detail:
"The Lord God formed man of dust from the ground, and
breathed into his nostrils the breath of life; and man became a
living being." This verse is vital to our discussion for it states
that God created man first and in a significantly different
manner than woman.

Genesis 2:18-23 expands on 1:27-28, adding some perti-
nent details in the process. After placing man in the Garden
of Eden, commanding him to cultivate it and not to eat from

the tree of the knowledge of good and evil (2:15-17), God said, "It is not good for the man to be alone; I will make him a helper suitable for him" (2:18). So He created Eve to assist Adam in ruling an undefiled world: "The Lord God caused a deep sleep to fall upon the man, and he slept; then He took one of his ribs, and closed up the flesh at that place. And the Lord God fashioned into a woman the rib which He had taken from the man, and brought her to the man" (vv. 21-22).

Upon meeting his wife, awestruck Adam declared, "This is now bone of my bones, and flesh of my flesh; she shall be called Woman, because she was taken out of Man" (v. 23). Immediately Adam recognized her as his perfect companion. He saw no blemishes or shortcomings in her, because both her character and his attitude were pure. There was nothing to criticize in Eve and there was no critical spirit in Adam.

The chapter concludes, "For this cause a man shall leave his father and his mother, and shall cleave to his wife; and they shall become one flesh. And the man and his wife were both naked and were not ashamed" (vv. 24-25). They were unashamed because no evil, impure, or perverse thoughts could exist in their perfect state.

Since man was created first, he was given headship over the woman and creation. The fact that Adam named Eve—a privilege bestowed on those who had authority in the Old Testament—manifested his authority over her. But their original relationship was so pure and perfect that his headship over her was a manifestation of his consuming love for her, and her submission to him was a manifestation of her consuming love for him. No selfishness or self-will marred their relationship. Each lived for the other in perfect fulfillment of their created purpose and under God's perfect provision and care.

Raymond C. Ortlund, Jr., professor at Trinity Evangelical Divinity School, explains succinctly the paradox of these two accounts:

> Was Eve Adam's equal? Yes and no. She was his spiritual equal and . . . "suitable for him." But she was not his equal in that she was his "helper." God did not create

man and woman in an undifferentiated way, and their mere maleness and femaleness identify their respective roles. A man, just by virtue of his manhood, is called to lead for God. A woman, just by virtue of her womanhood, is called to help for God ("Male-Female Equality and Male Headship," *Recovering Biblical Manhood and Womanhood,* 102).

How do evangelical feminists fix Genesis 2 to accommodate their prejudice? Specifically, how do they deal with the phrase "helper suitable for him"? Aida Besançon Spencer, an ordained minister in the Presbyterian Church, claims that the Hebrew word *neged,* which could be translated "in front of" or "in sight of," seems to suggest superiority or equality *(Beyond the Curse* [Peabody, Mass.: Hendrickson, 1989], 24). Ortlund, on the other hand, says that *neged* is accurately paraphrased as "a helper corresponding to him," hence the translation "suitable" *(Recovering Biblical Manhood and Womanhood,* 103). Spencer boldly concludes that "God created woman to be 'in front of' or 'visible' to Adam, which would symbolize equality (if not superiority!) in all respects. Even more, one can argue that the female is the helper who rules over the one she helps!" *(Beyond the Curse,* 25)

God did not create Eve to be superior to Adam; neither did He design her to be his slave. He did give them a perfect relationship: man as the head willingly providing for her, and she willingly submitting to him. Adam saw Eve as one with him in every respect—that was God's design for a perfectly glorious union.

SIN AND THE CURSE

But something terrible happened to God's beautiful design. Genesis 3:1-7 describes the first sin:

The serpent was more crafty than any beast of the field which the Lord God had made. And he said to the woman, "Indeed, has God said, 'You shall not eat from any tree of the garden'?" And the woman said to the serpent, "From the fruit of the trees of the garden we may eat; but from the fruit of the tree which is in the middle of the garden, God has said, 'You shall not eat from it or touch it, lest you die.' " And the serpent said to the woman, "You surely shall not die! For God knows that in the day you eat from it your eyes will be opened, and you will be like God, knowing good and evil." When the woman saw that the tree was good for food, and that it was a delight to the eyes, and that the tree was desirable to make one wise, she took from its fruit and ate; and she also gave to her husband with her, and he ate. Then the eyes of both of them were opened, and they knew that they were naked; and they sewed fig leaves together and made themselves loin coverings.

Bypassing the leadership of the man, the serpent went after the woman, who was by design the follower. He promised Eve that if she ate the forbidden fruit she would not die as God had warned, but that, in fact, she would become a god herself (vv. 4-5). He succeeded in enticing her to eat from the tree of the knowledge of good and evil. She in turn persuaded Adam to commit the same sin, thereby making Satan's attack on Adam's headship a success.

Eve sinned not only in disobeying God's specific command but also in acting independently of her husband by failing to consult him about the serpent's temptation. Adam sinned not only by disobeying God's command but also by succumbing to Eve's usurpation of his leadership, thus failing to exercise his God-given authority. Both the man and the woman twisted God's plan for their relationship, reversing their roles—and marriage has not been the same since.

Ortlund makes a perceptive observation: "Isn't it striking that we fell upon an occasion of sex role reversal? . . . Are we to institutionalize it in evangelicalism in the name of the God who condemned it in the beginning?" *(Recovering Biblical Manhood and Womanhood,* 107)

Elements of the Curse
Adam and Eve's sin precipitated a curse that affects the most basic elements of life:

- Death (Gen. 2:17): God warned Adam, "In the day that you eat from [the tree of the knowledge of good and evil] you shall surely die."
- Pain in childbearing (3:16): The wonderful reality and joy of having a child would be somewhat overshadowed by the anguish of childbirth.
- Strenuous work (3:17-19): Man was cursed with hard work, trouble, and frustration in eking out a living to provide for his family.
- Strife in marriage (3:16): As a consequence of Eve's disobedience and her failure to consult Adam about the serpent's temptation, God told her, "Your desire shall be for your husband, and he shall rule over you." I believe that aspect of the curse predicts marital strife brought on by a husband's oppressive rule over his wife and a wife's desire to dominate and lead their relationship (an interpretation suggested by Susan Foh in *Women and the Word of God* [Phillipsburgh, N.J.: P&R, 1979], 68–69).

The Hebrew word translated "rule" means "to reign." In the Septuagint (the Greek translation of the Old Testament) the word used means "to elevate to an official position." It's as if God were saying to the woman, "You were once co-regents, wonderfully ruling together as a team, but from now on the man is installed over you." That was not in God's original plan for man's headship. Although Scripture doesn't give us enough information to be dogmatic about what that rule means, the implication is that it represented a new, despotic authoritarianism.

The word "desire" in "your desire shall be for your husband" is difficult to translate. It couldn't be sexual or psychological—both characterize Adam's desire for Eve before the Fall. It is the same desire spoken of in the next chapter, however, where the identical Hebrew word is used. The term comes from an Arabic root that means "to compel," "to impel," "to urge," or "to seek control over." In Genesis 4:7 God essentially warns Cain, "Sin desires to control you, but you must master it." Sin wanted to master Cain, but God commanded Cain to master sin. Based on linguistic and thematic parallels between this verse and Genesis 3:16, the latter may be translated, "Your desire will be to control your husband, but he will rule over you." The curse on Eve was that woman's desire would henceforth be to usurp man's headship, yet he would resist that desire and subdue it through brutish means.

Effects of the Curse

With the Fall and its curse came the distortion of woman's proper submissiveness and of man's proper authority. That is where the battle of the sexes began, where women's liberation movements and male chauvinism were born. Women have a sinful inclination to usurp man's authority and men have a sinful inclination to put women under their feet. The divine decree that man would rule over woman in this way was part of God's curse on humanity. The unredeemed nature of both men and women is self-preoccupied and self-serving—characteristics that can only destroy rather than support harmonious relationships. Only a manifestation of grace in Christ through the filling of the Holy Spirit can restore the created order and harmony of proper submission in a relationship corrupted by sin.

Throughout history the most dominant distortion of relationships has occurred on the man's side. In most cultures of the ancient world, women were treated as little more than servants, and that practice is reflected in many parts of the world today. Marcius Cato, the famous Roman statesman of the second century B.C., wrote, "If you catch your wife in an act of infidelity, you can kill her without a trial. But if she were to catch you, she would not venture to touch you with her finger. She has no rights." That reflects the extreme of male ruthlessness resulting from the curse and exhibits the perversion of roles and responsibilities God intends for husbands and wives.

Even in supposedly liberated societies, women are frequently viewed primarily as sex objects who exist for the sensual pleasures of men. Because modern man is inclined to see himself as merely a higher form of animal—with no divine origin, purpose, or accountability—he is even more disposed to treat other people simply as things to be used for his own pleasure and advantage.

On the other hand, in today's society, it is feminine aggression that is taking its place as the dominant expression of the curse. Modern feminists are beginning to assert their rebellion against the divine order by mimicking the very *worst* traits of fallen males—brutality, cruelty, love of power, and a swaggering, macho arrogance.

While Satan's initial attack on God's supreme creation corrupted the family, sin also ushered in widespread alien, divisive influences. The Book of Genesis catalogs fratricide (4:8), polygamy (4:19, 23), evil sexual thoughts and words (9:22), adultery (16:1-4), homosexuality (19:4-11), fornication and rape (34:1-2), incest (38:13-18), prostitution (38:24), and seduction (39:7-12)—each of which directly attacks the sanctity and harmony of marriage and the family.

Satan knows by experience that when the home is weakened, all of society is weakened, because the heart of all human relationships is the family. The curse hits mankind at the core of its most needed human relationship: the need for men and women to help each other live productive, meaningful, and happy lives. But the rebellion against the divine order has promoted serving and indulging *self* as the key to finding meaning and happiness in life. Our culture encourages men and women to feel free to express sexual desire however they want—through promiscuity, unfaithfulness in marriage, partner swapping, homosexuality, bestiality, or whatever. When they take that deceptive bait, they join Satan in undermining and destroying every meaningful and truly satisfying relationship in their lives, receiving destruction and disease as the duly God-ordained consequence of such sins.

THE FEMINIZATION OF THE CHURCH

While Satan's attack on God's design for men and women is clear, another form is subtle and less obvious. Throughout history Satan has developed religious systems that counterfeit God's plan. Not surprisingly, some of them overturn God's pattern for the roles of men and women. One heresy in particular—Gnosticism—has had a profound influence not only on secular feminism, but evangelical feminism as well.

The Ancient Roots of Feminism

The current agenda is nothing more than a repackaging and reincarnation of ancient Gnosticism. Peter Jones, professor of New Testament at Westminster Theological Seminary, to whom I am indebted for the following material, explains that Gnosticism is a broad term describing a false anti-God religion developed "as the meeting of the mysticism of ancient Eastern religions with the rational culture of the Greek West" *(The Gnostic Empire Strikes Back* [Phillipsburg, N.J.: P&R, 1992], 15; Hans Jonas, *The Gnostic Religion* [Boston: Beacon Press, 1963], 23). Gnosticism took the intuitive, esoteric experiences of mystics and said this is a form of secret knowledge unknown to the uninitiated, but superior to biblical truth. The Bible, it claimed, is mundane, earthy, and incomplete.

Gnostic religion today comes under the term *New Age,* but there's nothing *new* about it. At the heart of ancient Gnosticism was a central myth: The physical universe was never intended to exist. Instead, we were meant to float around in the mystical free world of spirit life, unencumbered by physical definition and confinement. That's nothing more than the heresy of philosophical dualism — the assumption that matter is evil and spirit is good.

But the physical universe did come into being because, the ancient Gnostics claim, the foolish creator god of the Bible made a mistake and created it. To make their system work, Gnostics attempted to discredit the Creator by claiming He was an impostor, masquerading as the true, unknowable God. To make themselves more than just accidental protoplasm, the Gnostics said that when He created the universe, somehow He also accidentally infused into humanity a spark of divine life. Believing conveniently that they were divine yet imprisoned in evil matter, Gnostics had to release the divine within them through attaining intellectual and spiritual enlightenment. The way to accomplish this liberation was to rid themselves of the strictures of the Old Testament.

Ancient Gnosticism not only blasphemed God and rejected biblical truth, but also perverted the role of women — claiming, for example, that Eve was a spirit-endowed woman who saved Adam. Convoluting the account of the Creation and the

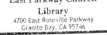
East Parkway Church
Library
4700 East Roseville Parkway
Granite Bay, CA 95746

Fall, gnostic texts say that Dame Wisdom was the Heavenly Eve—that she entered the snake in the Garden and taught both Adam and Eve the true way of salvation. Thus the snake is not the tempter; he is the instructor. He is also the redeemer—the true Christ, the true reflection of God.

Everything in gnostic literature displays a total reversal of redemptive history: The Creator God of Scripture is evil, the serpent in the Garden is the true Christ, and the Christ of the New Testament, as the reflection of God, is equally evil. Gnostics also claimed that since the true Christ never died, there was no resurrection. Thus redemption is not a gracious, miraculous transformation of a person through the sacrifice of Christ. Instead only self-understanding and self-realization can effect true redemption. Jones writes,

> Gnostic believers are "saved" when they realize who they are—a part of the divine; possessing within themselves the kingdom; capable of anything; and untrammeled by human traditions, creational structures, or divine laws. It follows that part of self-redemption is the rejection of biblical ethical norms and the promotion of the distortion of biblical sexuality (*The Gnostic Empire Strikes Back*, 26).

In the gnostic system, sexual roles are totally altered. In one ancient text the "divine revealer" says, "I am androgynous. I am both mother and father." Androgyny is the wiping out of all sexual distinction, a satanic goal from the beginning. June Singer, a Jungian analyst and avowed feminist, says, "Androgyny refers to a specific way of joining the 'masculine' and 'feminine' aspects of a single human being" *(Androgyny: Toward a New Theory of Sexuality* [Garden City, N.Y.: Anchor Press, 1976], 22). In her chapter on Gnosticism, notice how she links androgyny to the goal of Gnosticism: "Androgyny is the act of becoming more conscious and therefore more whole—because only by discovering and rediscovering ourselves in *all* of our many aspects, do we increase the range and quality of our consciousness" (pp. 134–35, emphasis in original). The ideal for the Gnostic is to become sexless—a radical refusal of sexual differentiation and a complete confusion of sexual identity in God's intended role.

The heart of Gnosticism and the New Age movement is that female power is the key to salvation, hence the current New Age emphasis on goddess power. Shirley MacLaine dedicates her book *Going Within* (New York: Bantam, 1989) to "Sachi, Mother, Kathleen and Bella and all the other women and men who seek the spiritual feminine in themselves" (Jones, 49). Male is the equivalent of matter and evil, whereas female is equated with spirit and good.

This heresy has influenced many who have some sort of Christian heritage. "I found God in myself and I loved her fiercely," says Roman Catholic theologian Carol Christ (Jones, 55; "Why Women Need the Goddess: Phenomenological, Psychological and Political Reflections," in Christ and Plaskow, *Womanspirit Rising: A Feminist Reader in Religion* [San Francisco: Harper and Row, 1979], 277). Vice President Al Gore, a Southern Baptist, expresses "his belief in the connectedness of all things, in the great value of all religious faiths, and in his hope that ancient pagan goddess worship will help bring us planetary and personal salvation" (Jones, 99–100; Gore, *Earth in the Balance: Ecology and the Human Spirit* [New York: Houghton Mifflin, 1992], 258–60).

Jones expresses well the goal of New Age theology when he writes, "The road to [the] perfect androgynous balance involves the destruction of the traditional male-female differentiation via sexual alternatives and New Age feminism" (p. 61). He offers as an example New Age author Charlene Spretnak's book *The Politics of Women's Spirituality* published by Doubleday in 1992. The book calls for an end to "Judeo-Christian religion by a feminist movement nourished on goddess-worship paganism, and witchcraft that succeeds in overthrowing the global rule of men" (Jones, 61).

In *The Feminization of America* (Los Angeles: Jeremy P. Tarcher, Inc., 1985), authors Elinor Lenz and Barbara Myerhoff celebrate this search for a new spirituality:

Feminine spirituality is a modern mystical journey, a quest for self-definition and integration with the powers of the universe. . . . Its authority resides within the individual, and since it recognizes no division between body and spirit, it blends sensual, earthy, erotic elements with spiritual reverence and personal mastery.

As a religion of process and synthesis, it is a faith for our time, for this dynamic, pluralistic, interdependent era when people need to find meaning and coherence within the human community rather than in some supernatural, all-powerful father god-figure. As the old gods die off and the new spirituality replaces them, we can look forward to a "third coming" that will help us achieve more fulfilling personal lives through a spiritual connection with others sharing our common humanity, with the divine mystery of creation, and with the natural world (pp. 155–56).

Sadly, undiscerning Christians are falling victim to these hellish heresies, and the church, instead of restraining this destructive force, is actually jumping on the bandwagon. David J. Ayers, assistant professor of sociology at Dallas Baptist University, explains, "Such a celebration of the feminine as a new spiritual force is not simply part of the backwaters of feminism. It has found a respected place within the mainstream feminist social agenda and is strongly evident as a growing movement within Christianity, including evangelicalism" ("The Inevitability of Failure: The Assumptions and Implementations of Modern Feminism," in *Recovering Biblical Manhood and Womanhood,* 322; see also Patricia Aburdene and John Naisbitt, *Megatrends for Women: From Liberation to Leadership* [New York: Fawcett Columbine, 1992], 267–88 for a detailed analysis of the Goddess movement as the spiritual arm of modern feminism).

For the past several hundred years Western society has been bombarded with the humanistic, egalitarian, sexless, classless philosophy that was the dominant force behind the French Revolution. Satan continues to mastermind the blurring and even total removal of all human distinctions with the goal of undermining legitimate, God-ordained authority in every realm of human activity — in government, the family, the school, and even in the church. We find ourselves continually victimized by the godless, atheistic concepts of man's supreme independence from every external law and any divine authority. The philosophy is self-destructive, because no group of people can live in orderliness and productivity if they reject God's Word and if each person is bent on doing his own will.

Much of the church, unfortunately, has fallen prey to this humanistic philosophy and is now willing to recognize the agenda of feminism and homosexuality in the ordination of women and homosexuals. It is usually argued that the biblical texts that are contrary to modern egalitarianism were uninspired or inserted by biased editors, scribes, prophets, or apostles. Bible interpreters function on the basis of a hermeneutic that is guided by contemporary humanistic philosophy rather than the absolute authority of Scripture as God's inerrant Word. The church is reaping the whirlwind of confusion, disorder, immorality, and apostasy that such denial of God's Word always spawns. We shouldn't expect anything less. After all, the Apostle Peter warned,

> False prophets also rose among the people, just as there will also be false teachers among you, who will secretly introduce destructive heresies, even denying the Master who bought them, bringing swift destruction upon themselves. And many will follow their sensuality, and because of them the way of truth will be maligned; and in their greed they will exploit you with false words (2 Peter 2:1-3).

The Apostle Paul encountered the same heresies in the first century. In the remaining chapters we will examine how he confronted the false teaching of his day and what he taught about God's design for men and women.

CHAPTER 2

The Case for Authority and Submission

No other author of Scripture has been attacked more often than the Apostle Paul. In the arena of male and female roles in the church, the most surprising attacks come not from secular feminists, but evangelical feminists. They often charge the apostle with being a male chauvinist, who frequently taught his own prejudices instead of God's Word.

Dr. H. Wayne House, associate professor of systematic theology at Dallas Theological Seminary and chairman of the Council on Biblical Manhood and Womanhood, writes,

Are we to ignore Paul's arguments that sin came from one man simply because we prefer a model of interpretation formulated by contemporary, atheistic anthropology over traditional interpretation? Likewise, should we refuse to believe in sin because we imagine that Paul merely borrowed his ideas on original sin from rabbinical theology?

Obviously, most evangelicals would answer these questions with a resounding "No!" Yet when the cases presented by many Christian feminists are distilled to their essence, these hypothetical examples are not much different than feminist arguments concerning other Pauline instruction. In such cases, the real question is whether or not all of the Bible is the authoritative, inerrant Word of God, and whether or not one will be submissive to it *(The Role of Women in Ministry Today* [Nashville: Thomas Nelson, 1990], 20–21).

That astute observation hits at the core of what evangelical feminists must do to reach their preconceived conclusions: compromise the inerrancy and infallibility of God's Word through disturbing methods of interpretation, such as "adopting novel views of the meanings of words and of grammatical and textual factors [that] if used in other areas of theology would probably be considered forced, if not clearly erroneous" *(The Role of Women in Ministry Today,* 29). One of the Scripture passages most frequently attacked is 1 Corinthians 11:3-16, and in particular the traditional interpretation of the Greek word translated "head" in verse 3 as meaning "authority over" — a word evangelical feminists must redefine to achieve their position. Let's look at that passage.

FEMINISM IN CORINTH

The Corinthian church faced the same problem as the contemporary church: a misunderstanding of male/female roles and relationships. Their confusion resulted from various feminist movements rampant in the Roman Empire during New Testament times. According to Juvenal women joined in men's hunts "with spear in hand and breasts exposed, and took to pig-sticking." He went on to write, "What modesty can you expect in a woman who wears a helmet, abjures her own sex, and delights in feats of strength?" *(Satires* 1.22–23, 61–62; 6.246–64)

In Corinth, women demanded the same treatment as men. Similar to many women today, they regarded marriage and the raising of children as unjust restrictions of their rights.

They resented bearing children for fear it would spoil their looks. Asserting their independence, they left their husbands and homes, refused to care for the children they did have, lived with other men, demanded jobs traditionally held by men, wore men's clothing and hairstyles, and discarded all signs of femininity.

Feminism gained its popularity primarily from the inhumane treatment women endured in that society. Most women were treated as nothing more than lowly slaves or animals, and husbands often bought, traded, or even disposed of their wives at will. Many Jewish women faced similar obstacles. Divorce was easy and commonplace, and it could be initiated almost exclusively by the husband. Some Jewish men held women in such low esteem that they developed a popular prayer in which they thanked God that they were not born a slave, a Gentile, or a woman.

In the midst of that culture Paul addresses the believers in Corinth regarding their apparent questions regarding the submission of women. He begins by explaining that woman's submission to man is but a reflection of God's general principle of authority and submission.

INDISPENSABLE ELEMENTS

Authority and submission characterize not only all of creation, but the Creator as well. Paul says, "Christ is the head of every man, and the man is the head of a woman, and God is the head of Christ" (1 Cor. 11:3). If Christ had not submitted to the will of God, redemption for mankind would have been impossible, and we would be lost forever. If individuals do not submit to Christ as Savior and Lord, they will be doomed for rejecting God's gracious provision. And if women do not submit to men, the family and society as a whole will be destroyed. Whether on a divine or human scale, submission and authority are indispensable elements in God's order and design.

Before instructing the Ephesians on how authority and submission should characterize their specific relationships (cf. Eph. 5:22ff), Paul emphasized the general attitude when he said, "Be subject to one another in the fear of Christ"

(v. 21). "Be subject" translates the Greek word *hupotassō*, originally a military term meaning "to arrange" or "to rank under." It expresses the relinquishing of one's rights to another. Paul counseled the Corinthian believers, for example, to be in subjection to their faithful ministers "and to everyone who helps in the work and labors" (1 Cor. 16:16). Peter commands us to "submit [ourselves] for the Lord's sake to every human institution" (1 Peter 2:13). A nation cannot function without rulers, soldiers, police, and others in leadership. That's not to say they are inherently superior to other citizens, but leaders are necessary for maintaining law and order to prevent the nation from falling into a state of anarchy. *WITHOUT FATHERS' LEADERSHIP IN HOME IT WILL FALL INTO ANARCHY AS WELL.*

Likewise within the church we are to "obey [our] leaders, and submit to them; for they keep watch over [our] souls, as those who will give an account" (Heb. 13:17). As is true with leaders in government, church leaders are not inherently superior to other Christians. But no institution — including the church — can function without a system of authority and submission.

In the home, the smallest unit of human society, the same principle applies. Even a small household cannot function if each member fully demands and expresses his own will. The system of authority God has ordained for the family is the headship of husbands over wives and of parents over children.

Since the "head" is the ruling part of the body, Paul used it figuratively to describe authority. The Greek word *kephalē* is translated "head" both in 1 Corinthians 11:3 and Ephesians 5:23. Throughout history Christians have always understood the word to mean "authority over." In recent years, however, certain feminists and scholars, in an effort to substantiate their desire for egalitarianism, have suggested it means "source" or "origin."

Using questionable writings of the classical Greek period as a basis, these writers claim that the use of *kephalē* to mean "authority over" would have been unclear to anyone living in the first century. One of the leading feminists who takes this position is Catherine Clark Kroeger in a work her supporters consider the last word on this issue ("The Classical Concept of *Head* as 'Source,' " in Appendix III in *Equal to Serve,* by Gretchen Gaebelein Hull [Old Tappan, N.J.: Fleming H. Revell, 1987], 267–83). But Wayne Grudem, in his excellent effort, "The Meaning of *Kephalē* ('Head'): A Response to Recent Studies" (Appendix 1 in *Recovering Biblical Manhood and Womanhood* [Wheaton, Ill.: Crossway, 1991], 425–68), identifies these so-called "classical" sources as originating from the fourth century A.D. and later. He concludes: "After all the research on this word ... there is still one unanswered question: Where is even one example of *kephalē* used of a *person* to mean 'source' in all of Greek literature before or during the time of the New Testament? Is there even *one* example that is unambiguous?" (p. 465, emphasis in original) He goes on to show that when *kephalē* is used figuratively, it always conveys the idea of authority over.

THE CLARIFICATION OF AUTHORITY
To help the Corinthians understand the principle of headship, Paul gives three examples in which it is manifested.

The Authority of Christ
Since "Christ is the Head of every man," He is uniquely the Head of the church as its Savior and Lord, having redeemed and bought it with His own blood. But in His divine authority Christ is Head of every human being, believer and nonbeliever alike. "All authority has been given to Me in heaven and on earth," Jesus declared (Matt. 28:18). Those who willingly submit to His authority are the church, and those who rebel against His authority are the world. READ INCOMPLETE CONTEXT REFFRS TO OUR EQUALITY AS BELIEVERS IN JESUS

The Authority of the Man
Paul next states that "the man is the head of a woman" (1 Cor. 11:3). As clear as this is, feminists often appeal at this point to Galatians 3:28 ("there is neither male nor female") to disprove the notion that husbands are to have authority over their wives and that wives should be submissive to their husbands—not to mention that women in general are to be submissive to men in general. Galatians 3:28 is so crucial to

their agenda that they consider it the "acid test" that proves functional equality between men and women. They claim Paul contradicted his teaching elsewhere in the New Testament, and that Galatians 3:28 is "his highest inspiration and his other teaching represents a reversion to his preconversion, rabbinic prejudice" (J. David Pawson, *Leadership Is Male* [Nashville: Thomas Nelson, 1990], 67). Closer examination of the context confirms that Paul was neither contradictory nor supportive of functional equality between men and women.

After reviewing the historical relationship and the redemptive superiority of the Abrahamic Covenant over the Law of Moses in Galatians 3:6-22, Paul introduces the personal application of the two covenants. In so doing he describes a person's condition before and after conversion: Before conversion he is under bondage to the Law; after conversion he is free in Christ. As Paul unfolds the aftereffects of salvation through faith in Christ, he describes three aspects of the believer's newfound freedom: he is a son of God (v. 26), one with every other believer (v. 28), and an heir of the promise (v. 29).

The key to the purpose in this book is the second aspect of freedom in Christ: we are one with other believers. Paul writes, "There is neither Jew nor Greek, there is neither slave nor free man, there is neither male nor female; for you are all one in Christ Jesus" (v. 28).

Dr. Robert L. Saucy offers an insightful interpretation of this pivotal verse:

> The interpretive question is: What is the distinction between male and female which is overcome in Christ? To phrase it another way in light of the apostle's statement "for you are all one in Christ Jesus," what is the "oneness" which male and female share in Christ? We would like to suggest . . . that the answers to these questions do not concern the functional order between man and woman at all. Rather the issue, as in the other two pairs mentioned [Jews and Greeks, slaves and freemen], concerns spiritual status before God. . . . To impart the is-

sue of the functional orders of human society into this
passage is to impute a meaning not justified by a valid
contextual exegesis. There is therefore no more basis
for abolishing the order between man and woman in the
church from Galatians 3:28 than for abolishing an order
between believing parents and children or believing citizens and rulers. For they are all one in Christ in or out
of the organization of the church ("The Negative Case
Against the Ordination of Women," in Kenneth S.
Kantzer and Stanley N. Gundry, eds., *Perspectives on
Evangelical Theology* [Grand Rapids: Baker, 1979],
281–82).

Their oneness in Christ did not obliterate the distinctions
between Jews and Gentiles. Nor did it remove the functional
differences between slaves and masters (cf. 1 Cor. 7:20-24).
Why, then, should we assume it did so between men and
women? That interpretation is further strengthened, Dr.
Saucy notes, by the use of the general terms "male" and
"female." In every Pauline passage dealing with functional
roles, the terms "man" and "woman," or "husband" and
"wife" appear. He writes, "Why, if the apostle is speaking of
the functional relationship in Galatians 3:28, does he not use
the language which he uses in every other passage? Why
does he not say, 'there is neither man nor woman' in Christ
rather than 'male' and 'female'?" (p. 283)

Those well-defined distinctions in the society of Paul's day
drew sharp lines and set up high walls of separation between
people. The essence of those distinctions was the notion that
some people—namely Jews, free men, and males in general—were better, more valuable, and more significant than
others. But the Gospel destroys all such proud thinking. No
longer are there distinctions among those who belong to
Christ—all are one in Him. In spiritual matters there is to be
no racial, social, or sexual discrimination.

Yet there are Christians who are Jews, Gentiles, slaves,
free persons, men, and women. Obvious racial, social, and
sexual differences do exist among people. Paul, however, was
speaking of spiritual differences—differences in standing be-

fore the Lord, spiritual value, privilege, and worthiness. Consequently prejudice based on race, social status, sex, or any other superficial and temporary differences doesn't belong in the fellowship of Christ's church. All believers, without exception, "are all one in Christ Jesus." God grants spiritual blessings, resources, and promises equally to all who believe.

In recognizing believing women as the full spiritual equals of believing men, Christianity elevated women to a status they had never known before in the ancient world. In matters of rule in the home and in the church, God has established the headship of men, but in the dimension of spiritual possessions and privilege, there is absolutely no difference.

That's why Paul makes no distinction between men and women as far as abilities, intellect, maturity, or spirituality are concerned. In fact, some women are obviously superior to some men in those areas. But God established the principle of male authority and female submission for the purpose of order and complementation, not on the basis of any innate superiority of males. An employee may be more intelligent and more skilled than his boss, but a company cannot be run without submission to proper authority, even if some in management are not as competent as they should be. Church leaders are chosen from among the most spiritual men of the congregation, but other men in the church may be even more spiritual. Those who are not in positions of leadership are still called to submit to those who are.

A church may have some women who are better Bible students, theologians, and speakers than many of the men. But if those women are obedient to God's order and committed to His design, they will submit to male leadership and not usurp it.

The Authority of God

The third manifestation of authority and submission is that "God is the Head of Christ" (1 Cor. 11:3). Jesus was clear that He submitted Himself to His Father's will (John 4:34; 5:30; 6:38; cf. 1 Cor. 3:23; 15:24-28). Christ has never been — before, during, or after His incarnation — inferior in essence to the Father. But in His incarnation He willingly subordinated Himself to the Father in His role as Savior, humbling Himself in loving obedience so He could fulfill God's redemptive plan.

These three aspects of authority and submission are inseparable. Just as Christ is submissive to the Father, Christians are to be submissive to Christ and women are to be submissive to men. One part cannot be rejected without rejecting the others. Anyone rejecting the principle of woman's submission to man must reject Christ's submission to the Father and believers' submission to Christ.

Authority and submission in each of those cases is based on love, not tyranny. The Father sent Christ out of love, not coercion, to redeem the world; and the Son submitted to the Father out of love, not compulsion. Christ loves the church so much that He died for it. And He rules the church in love, not in tyranny. In response, the church submits to Him in love. Likewise, men in general and husbands in particular should exercise their authority in love, not in tyranny. Their authority is not based on any greater worth or ability, but simply on God's wise design and loving will. Women, in turn, are to respond in loving submission.

A SYMBOL OF SIGNIFICANCE

To apply the principle of authority and submission to the particular problem facing the Corinthians, Paul wrote,

> Every man who has something on his head while praying or prophesying, disgraces his head. But every woman who has her head uncovered while praying or prophesying, disgraces her head; for she is one and the same with her whose head is shaved. For if a woman does not cover her head, let her also have her hair cut off; but if it is disgraceful for a woman to have her hair cut off or her head shaved, let her cover her head (1 Cor. 11:4-6).

Here Paul is referring to activities of believers in ministry before the Lord and the public, where a clear testimony is essential. In general "praying" is talking to God about people, including ourselves, and "prophesying" is talking to people about God. One is vertical (man to God) and the other is horizontal (man to man), and they represent the two primary dimensions of believers' ministry.

Because 1 Corinthians 11:5 mentions women praying and prophesying, some believe Paul acknowledged the right of women to teach, preach, and lead in the public assembly of the church (although some would restrict that to giving a word of testimony or reading Scripture in public). But Paul does not establish the setting as the official service of worship in the church. It is likely he was referring to praying or prophesying in places other than the church gathering. That would certainly fit with the very clear directives in 1 Corinthians 14:34 and 1 Timothy 2:12. Commentator F.W. Grosheide says,

> The fact that the work of the prophets was for the benefit of the churches does not imply that their prophetic utterances were made or should be made only in the churches. On the contrary, the Scripture teaches other possibilities. . . . Of special importance is Acts 21:11f., where the activities of Agabus are not pictured as taking place in a meeting of the congregation. This leads us to the conclusion that Paul in ch. 11 speaks of a praying and a prophesying (of women) in public rather than in the meetings of the congregation (*Commentary on the First Epistle to the Corinthians,* The New International Commentary [Grand Rapids: Wm. B. Eerdmans Publishing Co., 1953], 251–52).

The New Testament places no restrictions on a woman's witnessing in public to others, even to a man. Nor does it prohibit women from taking nonleadership roles of praying with believers or for unbelievers. Likewise there are no prohibitions against teaching children and other women (cf. Titus 2:3-4; 1 Tim. 5:16). Women may have the gift of prophecy, as did Philip's four daughters (Acts 21:9), but they are not to prophesy in the meetings of the church where men are present.

Women may pray and prophesy within the boundaries of

God's revelation, and with a proper sense of submission. In doing so it is critical that they reflect God's order and not appear rebellious. Whenever and wherever it is appropriate for men and women to pray or prophesy, they should do so while maintaining a proper distinction between male and female. Every man should speak to or for the Lord clearly as a man, and every woman should speak to or for the Lord clearly as a woman. God does not want the distinction or the role to be blurred.

That's the reality Paul was communicating when he offered a cultural example in 1 Corinthians 11:4-6. He said a man "disgraces his head" if he "has something on his head while praying or prophesying." The phrase "has something on his head" literally means "down from the head," and would normally refer to a veil. No one in Corinth would have argued with that—wearing a head covering (or veil) would have been completely ridiculous for a man yet completely proper for a woman.

In Corinthian society a man's praying or prophesying without a head covering was a sign of his authority over women, who were expected to have their heads covered. Consequently, for a man to cover his head would be a disgrace, because it suggested a reversal of the proper relationships.

The same was true for a woman. In Paul's day numerous symbols were used to exhibit the woman's subordinate relationship to men, particularly of wives to husbands. Usually the symbol took the form of a head covering, and in the Greek-Roman world of Corinth the symbol apparently was a veil. In many Middle-Eastern countries today, for example, a married woman's veil indicates that she reserves her beauty and charms entirely for her husband and will not expose herself to other men. Similarly, in the culture of first-century Corinth, wearing a head covering while ministering or worshiping was a woman's way of showing her devotion and submission to her husband—and to God's order.

Apparently some women in the Corinthian church were not covering their heads while praying or prophesying. Feminist movements in that day likely influenced some of the women believers in Corinth and, as a sign of protest and independence, they refused to cover their heads at appropriate times. In fact, Paul said that a woman who prayed or prophesied with her head uncovered made her the "same with her whose head is shaved" (v. 5). In that day, only a prostitute or an extreme feminist rebel would shave her head. It's hard to believe any Christian woman would desire to be identified in such a manner until recalling that some today appear so worldly as to make the same comparison possible.

Ultimately there is nothing right or wrong in wearing or not wearing a head covering. But rebellion against God-ordained roles is wrong, and in Corinth women praying and prophesying with their heads uncovered confirmed their rebellion. The principle of women's subordination to men, not the particular mark or symbol of that subordination, was Paul's focus here.

THE IMAGE AND GLORY OF GOD

While covering the head appears to have been a customary symbol of subordination in Corinthian society, the principle of male headship is not a custom but an established fact of God's order and creation, and it should never be compromised. Because a covered head was a sign of subordination, Paul told the Corinthians,

> For a man ought not to have his head covered, since he is the image and glory of God; but the woman is the glory of man. For man does not originate from woman, but woman from man; for indeed man was not created for the woman's sake, but woman for the man's sake. Therefore the woman ought to have a symbol of authority on her head, because of the angels (1 Cor. 11:7-10).

As we saw in chapter 1, man was created in the moral, mental, and spiritual image of God. He was also uniquely created to bear the image of God as a ruler, since God gave him a particular sphere of sovereignty. We have also seen that while both men and women are created in God's image, Adam was created first (Gen. 2:7) and Eve was created later from part of Adam himself (vv. 21-22). Thus the man was given the dominion and authority over God's created world, and is by that fact the glory of God. From Genesis 3:16 we learn that after the Fall man's rule was strengthened. Consequently he is not to wear any symbol of subordination.

On the other hand, "woman is the glory of man." She was made to manifest man's authority and will just as man was made to manifest God's authority and will. The woman is vice-regent—she rules in the stead of man or carries out man's will, just as man is God's vice-regent and rules in His stead or carries out His will. Although woman is fully in the image of God, she is not directly the glory of God, as is man. She is, however, directly the glory of man, the indirect outshining of man's glory of God. Paul's point is that man reveals how magnificent a creature God can create from Himself, while woman shows how magnificent a creature God can make from a man (2:21-22).

Yet as far as saving and sanctifying grace is concerned, a woman enters just as deeply into communion with God as a man. She was made equally in the image of God, and that image is equally restored through faith in Jesus Christ. She will be as much like Jesus as any man when she sees her Lord face to face (1 Cor. 13:12). But her role in this temporal world is to submit to the direction of man, to whom God gave dominion.

To further defend that truth Paul points out that "man does not originate from woman, but woman from man" (11:8). Adam was created first and was given dominion over the earth before the woman was created from him. Adam gave her the name "Woman, because she was taken out of Man" (Gen. 2:23; cf. 1 Tim. 2:11-13).

The woman was created not only from man but also for man: "For indeed man was not created for the woman's sake, but woman for the man's sake" (1 Cor. 11:9). She is not intellectually, morally, spiritually, or functionally inferior to man, but she is unique from him. Her role is to defer to his leadership, protection, and care, and be "a helper suitable for him" (Gen. 2:20).

In 1 Corinthians 11:10 Paul draws a conclusion from the

local custom he cited: "Therefore the woman ought to have a symbol of authority on her head, because of the angels." Here Paul identifies the woman's head covering as a "symbol of authority," which refers to "authority" or "rightful power." In other words, the woman's covered head gave her the authority or right to pray and worship, since it demonstrated her submissiveness.

While that is understandable, why does Paul say that women are to have this symbol "because of the angels"? The "angels" Paul refers to are the holy angels—God's ministering angels—whose supreme characteristic is total and immediate obedience to God. Throughout Scripture God's holy angels are presented as creatures of great power, but they derive their power from God and submit it to Him. Thus they are the leading example of proper creaturely subordination.

These messengers are God's protectors of His church, and they stand perpetual guard over it. Therefore it is appropriate for a woman to give a culturally meaningful sign of subordination so that these most submissive of all creatures will not be offended. Since the angels were present at creation (Job 38:7) as witnesses of God's unique design for man and woman, they would be distressed by any violation of that order.

THE BALANCING TRUTH

If Satan cannot persuade men to deny or disregard God's Word, he will try to entice them to misinterpret it and carry it to extremes the Lord never intended. Lest men abuse their authority over women, Paul reminds them of their equality and mutual dependence: "In the Lord, neither is woman independent of man, nor is man independent of woman. For as the woman originates from the man, so also the man has his birth through the woman; and all things originate from God" (1 Cor. 11:11-12). Man's authority over woman is delegated to him by God to be used for His purposes and in His way. As a fellow creature, man has no innate superiority to woman and no right to use his authority tyrannically or selfishly. *Male chauvinism is no more biblical than feminism.* Both are perversions of God's plan.

As we learned from Galatians 3:28, all believers, whether

male or female, are in the Lord and alike under Him. Their
roles differ in function, but not in spirituality or importance.
That's why Paul says, "Neither is woman independent of
man, nor is man independent of woman." Men and women
are complementary in every way, but particularly in the
Lord's work do they function together as a divinely ordained
team. They serve each other and they serve with each other.
Man's proper authority does not make him independent of
woman, nor does her proper subordination make her alone
dependent. Neither is independent of the other; they are mutually dependent.

God created the first woman from the man, but since that
time every man is born through a woman (1 Cor. 11:12). That
is God's wise and gracious harmony and balance.

While women are not to be teachers of men, they are
usually the most influential shapers of men. Bearing and nurturing children saves women from any thought of lower status than men (1 Tim. 2:15). As mothers they have an indispensable role in training and developing a future generation
of men. From conception to adulthood a man is dependent on
and shaped by his mother in a unique and marvelous way.
And throughout adulthood, whether married or single, he is
dependent on women in more ways than he is often willing to
acknowledge. In marriage men cannot be faithful to the Lord
unless they are willingly and lovingly dependent on the wife
He has given them. In the Lord's work men cannot be faithful
to Him unless they are dependent on the women to whom
He has given responsibility in His church. They are perfect
complements — one the head, leader, and provider; the other
the helper, supporter, and companion.

REFLECTING ON THE NATURAL ORDER

The principle of authority and submission is not only based
on God's Word, but also observable in His creation. The
cultural practice of a woman's covering her head as a symbol
of subordination to man is a reflection of the natural order.
That's why Paul asks, "Does not even nature itself teach you
that if a man has long hair, it is a dishonor to him, but if a
woman has long hair, it is a glory to her?" (1 Cor. 11:14-15)

Men and women have distinctive physiologies. One obvious difference is the process of hair growth. Head hair develops in three stages: formation and growth, resting, and fallout. The male hormone testosterone speeds up the cycle so that men reach the third stage earlier than women. The female hormone estrogen causes the cycle to remain in stage one for a longer period, causing women's hair to grow longer than men's. Women are rarely bald because few ever reach stage three. This physiology is reflected in most cultures of the world when women wear their hair longer than men.

Beautiful hair is "a glory," God's special gift for displaying the softness and tenderness of a woman. It, like the Corinthian head covering, is a symbol of subordination to man and thus a reflection of the divine order. The unique beauty of a woman is gloriously manifest in the distinctive femininity portrayed by her hairstyle and sensitivity to other appropriate feminine customs of her society. Thus both nature and general custom reflect God's universal principle of man's role of authority and woman's role of subordination.

In cultures where the wearing of a veil or hat does not symbolize submission, that practice should not be required of Christians. But women's hair and dress is to be distinctively feminine. There should be no confusion about male and female identities since God has made the sexes distinct, both in physiology and in roles and relationships. He wants men to be masculine—to be responsibly and lovingly authoritative. He wants women to be feminine—to be responsibly and lovingly submissive.

The point of Paul's cultural illustration is that we should identify with *our* society's symbols of masculinity and femininity (unless, of course, they violate Scripture). Such symbols can be easily discerned. We can often determine by a woman's appearance if she is rebelling against everything that womanhood stands for, or if a man is effeminate and denying recognized symbols of masculinity.

In summary,

Gender must not be confused in gathering for worship. It is offensive to God (this is why homosexuality and transvestism are "abominations" to him) and is of significance . . . to the angels (verse 10), who also attend our services. The gender difference is to be visibly acknowledged (the sex of a worshiper should be perfectly obvious to a person in the pew behind!). For the woman, this expresses her acceptance of male governmental responsibility within the assembly. . . . For the man, it expresses his acknowledgement of the need to submit to the authority of Christ while he fulfills his role in the church (J. David Pawson, *Leadership Is Male* [Nashville: Thomas Nelson, 1990], 79).

As in almost every age and every church since, some of the believers in Corinth were not satisfied with God's design and wanted to disregard it or modify it to suit their agenda. Paul anticipated their objection to his teaching. He knew that some would be "inclined to be contentious" (1 Cor. 11:16), but he could say nothing more convincing than what he had already said: Women are to be submissive to men because it demonstrates the relationship between Christ and God (v. 3), sensitivity to their society (vv. 4-6), the order and purpose of their creation (vv. 7-9, 11-12), consideration of the angels (v. 10), and observable truths of natural physiology (vv. 13-15).

PART TWO

God's Design
for Marriage

CHAPTER 3

Marriage As It Was Meant to Be

During the 1992 Presidential campaign, former Vice President Dan Quayle made national headlines by accusing the producers of a popular television show of promoting single motherhood in one of their programs. His comments prompted a national debate on "family values" and much analysis on the state of the American family. One thing is clear, we are witnessing the death of the traditional family where the husband is the sole breadwinner and the wife remains at home to manage the household and raise the children. Marital infidelity, sexual sin, homosexuality, abortion, women's liberation, delinquency, and the sexual revolution in general have all contributed to the demise of this type of family.

During the past twenty-five years some sociologists and psychologists believed marriage ought to radically change or be eliminated altogether. That kind of "enlightened" thinking was based on the notion that marriage had failed to meet people's needs, and that men and women no longer needed

such an institution to live productive, satisfying lives. But
marriage hasn't failed—it's just that more and more people
are avoiding it. And of those who do marry, half eventually
bail out instead of exerting the consistent effort and determi-
nation necessary to make their marriages succeed.

Even secular thinkers observed this trend over twenty
years ago:

> The institution of marriage is most assuredly in an un-
> certain state. If 50 to 75 percent of Ford or General
> Motors cars completely fell apart within the early part of
> their lifetimes as automobiles, drastic steps would be
> taken. We have no such well organized way of dealing
> with our social institutions, so people are groping, more
> or less blindly, to find alternatives to marriage (which is
> certainly less than 50 percent successful). Living to-
> gether without marriage, living in communes, extensive
> child care centers, serial monogamy (with one divorce
> after another), the women's liberation movement to es-
> tablish the woman as a person in her own right, new
> divorce laws which do away with the concept of guilt—
> these are all gropings toward some new form of man-
> woman relationship for the future. It would take a bolder
> man than I to predict what will emerge (Carl Rogers,
> *Becoming Partners: Marriage and Its Alternatives* [New
> York: Dell, 1973], 11).

What has emerged is that marriage is in worse shape than
ever thanks to the failed social experiments. In the June 8,
1992 issue of *Newsweek,* Joe Klein updates us with these
sobering facts:

> Most Americans . . . have measured themselves (con-
> sciously or not) against "Ozzie and Harriet"—or some
> shimmering image of nuclear bliss—and come up short.
> . . . Only about a third of American families structurally
> resemble the Nelsons these days. The divorce rate re-
> mains, stubbornly, one out of two. The out-of-wedlock
> birthrate has tripled since 1970; it is among the

highest in the "developed" world. A nauseating buffet of dysfunctions has attended these trends—an explosion in child abuse, crime, learning disabilities, welfare dependency, name your pathology. . . .

Then there are the things Dan Quayle doesn't talk about: the allure of excess, the deluge of crass propaganda—buying is more important than giving, having is more important than being part of. It often seems that the sterile ceremonies of consumerism are the most profound rituals Americans share as a people. . . .

The disaster that has overtaken American families has been quieter, more diffuse, but—as the data begin to trickle in, the casualty reports from the sexual revolution—incontrovertible. . . . Karl Zinsmeister, a scholar at the American Enterprise Institute [says], "The data are monolithically worrisome. None of these circumstances—divorce, single-parent families, stepparent families—are healthy. There is no precedent for what has happened in any other time, in any other place." . . .

The numbers are daunting. There is a high correlation between disrupted homes and just about every social problem imaginable. According to research compiled by Zinsmeister, more than 80 percent of the adolescents in psychiatric hospitals come from broken families. Approximately three out of four teenage suicides "occur in households where a parent has been absent." A 1988 study by Douglas A. Smith and G. Roger Jaroura showed that "the percentage of single-parent households with [teenage] children . . . is significantly associated with rates of violent crime and burglary" ("Whose Values," 19–21).

If that's what the last twenty years brought, what will the next twenty bring? Can life as we know it get worse? Twenty centuries ago the Apostle Paul said it would:

Realize this, that in the last days difficult times will come. For men will be *lovers of self, lovers of money,* boastful, arrogant, revilers, *disobedient to parents,* un-

grateful, unholy, *unloving,* irreconcilable, malicious gossips, without self-control, brutal, haters of good, treach-
erous, reckless, conceited, *lovers of pleasure rather than
lovers of God.* . . . Evil men and impostors will proceed
from bad to worse, deceiving and being deceived (2 Tim.
3:1-4, 13, emphasis added).

Notice that the first traits of the last days are an overwhelming self-centeredness and self-indulgence – characteristics certainly true of our day. Our entertainment-conscious
society helps feed all sorts of illusions about reality. The
fantasy of the perfect romantic and sexual relationship, the
perfect lifestyle, and the perfect body all prove unattainable
because the reality never lives up to the expectation. The
worst fallout comes in the marriage relationship. When two
people can't live up to each other's expectations, they'll look
for their fantasized satisfaction in the next relationship, the
next experience, the next excitement. But that path leads
only to self-destruction and emptiness.

Two other iniquities Paul mentions directly undermine the
family: "disobedient to parents" and "unloving," which could
best be translated "without family affection." Homes characterized by a lack of love and disobedience are doomed to
produce children lacking respect and a proper perspective of
authority. And we're seeing the result in the rise in delinquency, suicide, and mental illness. Ultimately every sin
weakens the relationships between husband and wife, parents
and children, and brothers and sisters.

Since families are the building blocks of human society, a
society that does not protect the family undermines its very
existence. When the family goes, anarchy is the logical outcome – and that's where we're headed. Now, more than ever
before, is the time for Christians to declare and put on display
what the Bible declares: God's standard for marriage and the
family is the *only* standard that can produce meaning, happiness, and fulfillment.

If we are to impact the world with that standard, we must
be different. God has called us to be salt and light in this dark
and decaying society. Our responsibility is to a higher level of

living—to a new way of thinking, a new way of acting, a new way of living—to "walk in a manner worthy of the calling with which [we] have been called . . . [to] put on the new self, which in the likeness of God has been created in righteousness and holiness of the truth" (Eph. 4:1, 24). We cannot think as the world thinks, act as the world acts, talk as the world talks, or set goals the world sets—we must be distinct. The ultimate hope of humanity is that in seeing that distinction lost people will be drawn to Jesus Christ.

The Apostle Paul and the church at Ephesus faced a culture steeped in pagan ritual and tradition. In Greek society life was especially difficult for wives. Concubines were common and a wife's role was simply to bear legitimate children and keep house. Both male and female prostitution were rampant. Husbands typically found sexual gratification with concubines and prostitutes, whereas wives, often with the encouragement of their husbands, found sexual fulfillment with their slaves, both male and female. Prostitution, homosexuality, and the many other forms of sexual promiscuity and perversion inevitably resulted in widespread sexual abuse of children. Roman society was just as bad. Marriage was little more than legalized prostitution and divorce was an easily obtained formality.

In the setting of such an immoral world Paul admonished the believers in Ephesus with God's elevated and original divine standard for marriage: "For the husband is the head of the wife, as Christ also is the head of the church, He Himself being the Savior of the body. But as the church is subject to Christ, so also the wives ought to be to their husbands in everything. Husbands, love your wives, just as Christ also loved the church and gave Himself up for her" (5:23-25). The relationship between a husband and wife is to be holy and indissoluble, just like Christ's relationship with the church.

For that type of a relationship to be a reality, Christ must be at its center. The principles for marriage, while beneficial to the unredeemed, will have limited application for them. Only those who belong to God through faith in His Son will fully understand and apply the power and potential of those principles. Being subject to one another finds its power and effectiveness only in the fear of Christ (v. 22). The family can only be what God has designed it to be when the members of the family are what God designed them to be — "conformed to the image of His Son" (Rom. 8:29).

DIVINE DIRECTIVES FOR WIVES

Wives often bear the brunt of Ephesians 5:22-33, although the majority of the passage deals with the husband's attitude toward and responsibilities for his wife. I'm sure Ephesians 5:22, "Wives, submit yourselves unto your own husbands" (KJV), is etched in granite in many homes. There's a tendency for men to grab their wives and yell, "Submit!" But it is interesting to note that the verb translated "submit" has a softened force since it does not actually appear in the original Greek text — its meaning is implied from verse 21. Paul is commanding everyone to be subject to one another in the fear of Christ and, as the first example, wives are to be subject to their own husbands.

We noted in the previous chapter that "be subject" refers to a relinquishing of one's rights. In no way does it imply a difference in essence or worth; it does refer, however, to a willing submission of oneself. Wives, submission is to be your voluntary response to God's will — a willingness to give up your rights to other believers in general and ordained authority in particular, in this case your own husband.

Paul did not issue a command to wives to obey their husband, like he commanded children and slaves to obey their parents and masters (6:1, 5). Husbands aren't to treat their wives like slaves, barking commands; husbands are to treat their wives as equals, assuming their God-given responsibility of caring, protecting, and providing for them. Likewise wives fulfill their God-given responsibility when they submit willingly to their *own* husbands. That reflects not only the depth of intimacy and vitality in their relationship, but also the sense of ownership a wife has for her husband.

Both the mutual possessiveness and mutual submission of the husband/wife relationship is expressed beautifully in Paul's first letter to the Corinthians, where he made it clear that the physical relationships and obligations are not one-sided: "Let the husband fulfill his duty to his wife, and likewise also the wife to her husband. The wife does not have authority over her own body, but the husband does; and likewise also the husband does not have authority over his own body, but the wife does" (7:3-4). The husband no more possesses his wife than she possesses him. He is not superior and she is not inferior—they belong to each other.

In a parallel passage to Ephesians 5:22, Paul said, "Wives, be subject to your husbands, as is fitting in the Lord" (Col. 3:18). Paul used the same Greek word *(anēkō)* translated "as is fitting" in Philemon 8 in reference to something that was legally binding. The wife's submission to her husband is legally binding—it was the accepted standard of society. How ironic that such an accepted standard throughout history should be so thoroughly questioned in this century.

Ephesians 5:22 concludes that a wife is to be subject to her husband "as to the Lord." Everything we do for the Lord is to be done first of all for His glory and to please Him (1 Cor. 10:31). So when we submit to others, whether in mutual submission or to functional authority, we do it because it is the Lord's will and ultimately the submission is to Him. A wife who properly submits to her husband submits herself to the Lord.

Why? "For the husband is the head of the wife, as Christ also is the head of the church" (Eph. 5:23). The head gives the orders, the body doesn't. When a physical body responds appropriately to the mind, it is well-coordinated. But if the body doesn't respond, it is either crippled, paralyzed, or spastic. Likewise, a wife who doesn't respond properly to the direction of her husband manifests a serious spiritual dysfunction. A wife who responds willingly and lovingly, however, honors God, her husband, her family, her church, and herself. Additionally, she becomes a beautiful testimony of the Lord before the watching world.

Keep in mind that the wife's submission requires intelligent participation: "Mere listless, thoughtless subjection is not desirable if ever possible. The quick wit, the clear moral discernment, the fine instincts of a wife make of her a counselor whose influence is invaluable and almost unbounded"

(Charles R. Erdman, *The Epistles of Paul to the Colossians and to Philemon* [Philadelphia: Westminster, 1966], 103). That is only appropriate of one who was created to be the ideal complement and helper to her mate (cf. Gen. 2:18).

Since Christ is "the Savior of the body" (Eph. 5:23), He is the perfect Provider, Protector, and Head of His church. Thus He becomes the perfect role model for the husband, who is to be his wife's provider and protector. Wives are no more to be coproviders and coprotectors with their husbands than the church is to have such joint roles with Christ. The wife is to flourish under her husband's provision and protection. That's God's ordained pattern. When we follow it, we will have happier homes, godly children, and fewer divorces. God will be honored, and His Word will not be blasphemed.

Finally, verse 24 says that a wife is to subject to her husband "in everything." There's only one exception: If her husband tells her to do something contrary to Scripture, she must obey God (cf. Acts 5:29). The key to being that kind of wife is being "filled with the Spirit" (Eph. 5:18), which is analogous to letting "the word of Christ richly dwell within you" (Col. 3:16).

Elisabeth Elliot, writing on "The Essence of Femininity," offers a fitting summary of God's ideal for wives:

> Unlike Eve, whose response to God was calculating and self-serving, the virgin Mary's answer holds no hesitation about risks or losses or the interruption of her own plans. It is an utter and unconditional self-giving: "I am the Lord's servant.... May it be to me as you have said" (Luke 1:38). This is what I understand to be the essence of femininity. *It means surrender.*
>
> Think of a bride. She surrenders her independence, her name, her destiny, her will, herself to the bridegroom in marriage.... The gentle and quiet spirit of which Peter speaks, calling it "of great worth in God's sight" (1 Peter 3:4), is the true femininity, which found its epitome in Mary (John Piper, *Recovering Biblical Manhood and Womanhood* [Wheaton, Ill.: Crossway, 1991), 398, 532, emphasis added).

DIVINE DIRECTIVES FOR HUSBANDS

After giving the divine guidelines for the husband's leadership and the wife's submission, Paul devotes the next nine verses to explain the husband's duty to submit to his wife through his love for her: "Husbands, love your wives, just as Christ also loved the church" (Eph. 5:25). Obviously no sinful human being has the capacity to love with the divine perfection with which Christ loves the church. But believers do possess Christ's own nature and Holy Spirit, thus husbands can love their wives with a measure of Christ's own kind of love. The Lord's pattern of love for His church is the husband's pattern of love for his wife, and it is manifest in four ways.

Sacrificial Love

Christ loved the church by giving "Himself up for her." Romans 5:7-8 tells us about the depth of Christ's love for the church: "One will hardly die for a righteous man; though perhaps for the good man someone would dare even to die. . . . God demonstrates His own love toward us, in that while we were yet sinners [as well as enemies, v. 10], Christ died for us." No person deserves salvation, forgiveness, and a place in God's kingdom, but Christ made the greatest sacrifice for the most unworthy people. The contrast is incredible: An absolutely holy, righteous God made the greatest, most magnanimous sacrifice for the vilest of all people. Husbands, don't tell me about your wife's problems that make it hard to love her—you're not as far removed from your wife as God was from sinners, yet He loved you. Your wife may be a sinner, but so are you. Don't lose that perspective.

Men who explain away their difficult marriages by claiming they no longer love their wives are being disobedient to God's command. On the other hand, I heard about one man who feared he was loving his wife too much. When asked if he loved her as much as Christ loved the church, he answered, "No, not nearly as much." His friend replied, "Then you'd better love her more." The divine standard of love is infinitely high.

In contrast, the world loves with an object-oriented love:

Everything depends on the form of an object or its personality. It tends to be cliquish and overly selective, sins that can influence even Christians (e.g., James 2:1-13).

When such people desire a partner, they look for physical attractiveness, personality, wit, prestige, or some other such positive characteristic. But that love is necessarily fickle because the moment the characteristic that motivated the love disappears, or loses its appeal, the love disappears. Many marriages fall apart simply because the relationship was founded on that kind of love.

God's love is different. First, "there is no partiality with God" (Rom. 2:11), and second, He doesn't expect the object to be worthy; it's His nature to love that which He has created. John 3:16 says, "For God so loved the world." If God were going to love anything on the basis of its innate appeal, it would not have been the world. The world hated God, but God still loved the world.

Because God gave His children the capacity to love as He loves, He can command His love from them. That means love is a choice we make—it is an act of our will as well as our heart. Husbands, Scripture is not commanding you to love your wife because she deserves it but to love her even if she doesn't deserve it. Love isn't an issue of attraction; it's a binding commandment from God. When you choose to love someone who is no longer attractive to you, he or she will soon become attractive. Loving as Christ loves does not depend on what others are in themselves, but entirely on what we are in Christ.

That does not mean we should ignore the importance a wife's beauty, kindness, gentleness, or any other positive quality or virtue has in generating admiration from her husband. But while those qualities bring great blessing and enjoyment, they are not the bond of marriage. If every appealing characteristic and virtue of his wife were to disappear, a husband is still under obligation to love her. In fact he is under greater obligation because her need for the healing and restorative power of his selfless love is greater. That's the kind of love Christ has for His church and is therefore the kind of love every Christian husband is to have for his wife.

Love, as God defines it, is much more an action than an emotion (cf. John 13:3-34; 1 Cor. 13:4-7). The world says, "When the feeling stops, the love is over." That kind of "love" creates serial monogamy; it's not the love of the Bible. Divine love is an act of selfless sacrifice. When you love in that way, you'll do what is needed without counting the cost or analyzing the need's merit. And your love will continue to meet the need no matter if it is received or rejected, appreciated or resented.

The husband who loves his wife as Christ loves His church will give up everything he has for his wife, including his life if necessary. While most husbands give verbal assent to that (since that prospect is so remote for most husbands), I would speculate that it is much more difficult to make lesser, but actual, sacrifices for her. Husbands, when you put your own likes, desires, opinions, preferences, and welfare aside to please your wife and meet her needs, then you are truly dying to self to live for your wife. And that is what Christ's love demands.

To regularly remind myself of what it means to manifest self-sacrificing love, I keep on my desk the following words from an unknown source:

> When you are forgotten or neglected or purposely set at naught, and you sting and hurt with the insult of the oversight, but your heart is happy, being counted worthy to suffer for Christ — that is dying to self. When your good is evil spoken of, when your wishes are crossed, your advice disregarded, your opinions ridiculed and you refuse to let anger rise in your heart, or even defend yourself, but take it all in patient loving silence — that is dying to self. When you lovingly and patiently bear any disorder, any irregularity, or any annoyance, when you can stand face to face with waste, folly, extravagance, spiritual insensibility, and endure it as Jesus endured it — that is dying to self. When you are content with any food, any offering, any raiment, any climate, any society, any attitude, any interruption by the will of God — that is dying to self. When you never care to refer to yourself

in conversation, or to record your own good works, or itch after commendation, when you can truly love to be unknown—that is dying to self. When you see your brother prosper and have his needs met and can honestly rejoice with him in spirit and feel no envy nor question God, while your own needs are far greater and in desperate circumstances—that is dying to self. When you can receive correction and reproof from one of less stature than yourself, can humbly submit inwardly as well as outwardly, finding no rebellion or resentment rising up within your heart—that is dying to self.

Paul says that love "does not seek its own" (1 Cor. 13:5). Husbands, as long as you're looking for what you can get out of marriage, you will never know what it means to love your wife as Christ loved the church. Look instead for what you can give: Be willing to make personal sacrifices for your wife, considering her needs and interests before your own (Phil. 2:3-4).

Purifying Love

Christ loved the church sacrificially with this goal in mind: "That He might sanctify her, having cleansed her by the washing of water with the word, that He might present to Himself the church in all her glory, having no spot or wrinkle or any such thing; but that she should be holy and blameless" (Eph. 5:26-27). That is a purifying love, teaching us this basic truth: When you love someone, that person's purity is your goal. You can't love a person and at the same time want to defile him or her.

Christ's great love for His church does not allow Him to be content with any sin—with any moral or spiritual impurity. But He doesn't simply condemn wrong in those He loves; He seeks to cleanse them from it. As we continue to confess our sins, Christ "is faithful and righteous to forgive us our sins and to cleanse us from all unrighteousness" (1 John 1:9).

Love wants only the best for the one it loves, and it cannot bear for a loved one to be corrupted or misled by anything evil or harmful. Did you know that marrying your wife purified her by taking her out of the world and away from her past? Whatever relationships she may have had—whatever indulgences may have been involved—marriage sets her apart and purifies her. If you really love your wife, you'll do everything in your power to maintain her holiness, virtue, and purity every day you live. That obviously means doing nothing to defile her. Don't expose her to or let her indulge in anything that would bring impurity into her life. Don't tempt her to sin by, say, inducing an argument out of her on a subject you know is sensitive to her. An even worse situation is a husband who flirts with a secretary or a neighbor woman. If you do that you give your wife reason to feel rejected and lonely—and perhaps to begin flirting herself. What you have done is jeopardize not only your own moral purity, but your wife's as well, and you share the responsibility for any indiscretion or immorality in which she might be tempted to become involved. Love always seeks to purify.

In ancient Greece, a bride-to-be would be led to a river to be bathed and ceremonially cleansed from every defilement of her past life. That allowed her to enter marriage without any moral or social blemish—she was symbolically pure. But Christ's cleansing of believers is not ceremonial and symbolic; it is real and complete. He has cleansed the church "by the washing of water with the word, that He might present to Himself the church in all her glory, having no spot or wrinkle or any such thing; but that she should be holy and blameless" (Eph. 5:26-27). Saving grace makes believers holy through the cleansing agency of the Word of God, so that they may be presented to Christ as His pure bride, forever to dwell in His love. It is with the same purpose and in that same love that husbands are to cultivate the purity, righteousness, and sanctity of their wives.

Caring Love

Another aspect of divine love is this: "Husbands ought also to love their own wives as their own bodies. He who loves his own wife loves himself; for no one ever hated his own flesh, but nourishes and cherishes it, just as Christ also does the church" (vv. 28-29).

Men, we spend a lot of time on our bodies. We groom ourselves diligently, eat the best of foods, exercise when we can, and wear nice clothes. After all, a Christian's body is the temple of the Holy Spirit! (1 Cor. 6:19) We certainly don't want to mar it, so we take good care of it — or at least try. When your body has needs, you meet them. Your wife also has needs, and you're to meet them just as diligently. We have a sense of well-being when we are healthy, and when you meet the needs of your wife with the same care and concern you devote to yourself, you will also experience a sense of well-being as a by-product of your love.

The husband who loves his wife as Christ loves the church will no more do anything to harm her than he will harm his own flesh. His desire is to nourish and cherish her just as he "nourishes and cherishes" his own body — because that is how Christ also cares for the church.

When your wife needs strength, give her strength. When she needs encouragement, give her that. Whatever she needs, you are obligated to supply as best you can. Don't forget: You're her divinely ordained provider and protector, but should that responsibility ever overwhelm you, recall that God is *your* Provider and Protector. He will help you do all that He requires.

Some husbands view their wife as nothing more than a cook, baby-sitter, clothes-washer, and sex-partner. Don't be one of them. A wife is a God-given treasure to be cared for and cherished (cf. Prov. 18:22). The word translated "cherishes" in Ephesians 5:29 literally means "to warm with body heat." It is used to describe a bird sitting on her nest (e.g., Deut. 22:6). Husbands are to provide a secure, warm, safe haven for their wives. Don't shove your wife out into the cold, hard, cruel world.

Paul's warning to husbands in Colossians 3:19 is appropriate at this point: "Husbands, love your wives, and *do not be embittered* against them" (emphasis added). The love that existed from the beginning is to continue throughout the marriage; it must not give way to bitterness. Paul was well aware of the tendency for bitterness to encroach on a marriage, and that the husband is the primary — although not necessarily exclusive—avenue through which bitterness infiltrates.

"Do not be embittered" could be translated "stop being bitter" or "do not have the habit of being bitter." In its only other New Testament uses, it refers to something bitter in taste. Don't be harsh or resentful to your wife or allow yourself to be preoccupied with her flaws. She, like you, is bound to have plenty of them. Respond with patience and loving leadership instead of masculine pride or outrage.

What else does it mean? A couple of commentators offer these helpful observations:

> ● Christian love . . . should have a controlling influence on character and everyday living. Our life with those closest to us in the family circle is subjected to strains and stresses which we can easily brush off in less personal relationships in the outside world. How we act in the intimacy of the home and marriage circle is a true indication of the quality of our love as Christians. In a strange quirk of human behaviour we can often injure thoughtlessly those we love the most (Ralph P. Martin, *Colossians: The Church's Lord and the Christian's Liberty* [Grand Rapids: Zondervan, 1972], 130).

> ● Just as some wives may be united to tyrannical and unreasonable men, so there are husbands who, after marriage, find that one who in days of courtship seemed so docile and affectionate is . . . as unreasonable as it is possible to be. But still the husband is to love and care for her . . . without indulging in wrath or anger. . . . God knew how petty and trying some women's ways would be when He said to good men, "Be not bitter against them." In the power of the new life one may manifest patience and grace under the most trying circumstances (H.A. Ironside, *Lectures on the Epistle to the Colossians* [New York: Loizeaux Brothers, n.d.], 158–59).

Unbreakable Love

For a husband to love his wife as Christ loves His church he must love her with an unbreakable love. In this direct quota-

tion from Genesis 2:24, Paul emphasizes the permanence as
well as the unity of marriage: "For this cause a man shall
leave his father and mother, and shall cleave to his wife; and
the two shall become one flesh" (Eph. 5:31). God's standard
for marriage has not changed.

One great barrier to successful marriages is the failure of
one or both couples to "leave . . . father and mother." A new
family begins with a marriage, and while the relationships
between child and parents still exist, they are severed as far
as authority and responsibilities are concerned. You need to
love and care for your parents, but you cannot let them control your lives now that you're married. As a new husband
and wife, you are to leave your parents and "cleave" to—be
cemented to—each other. You break one set of ties and establish another set. And don't forget the second one is more
binding and permanent than the first.

Another barrier, and even more devastating, is divorce. " 'I
hate divorce,' says the Lord, the God of Israel" (Mal. 2:16).
He hates it because it destroys what He has ordained to be
unbreakable. With the high incidence of divorce in our society, it becomes tempting for Christian couples to bypass
God's Word and look to the world's so-called experts for
solutions. But their remedies often encourage Christian husbands and wives to divorce no matter what the wrong. As
Christians, however, we are not to be quick to divorce for
wrongs our spouses have done, not even for unfaithfulness.
Christ has set the standard. Just as Christ is always forgiving
of believers, husbands and wives should always be forgiving
of each other.

Though He has made provision for divorce in the cases of
unrepentant and continued adultery (Matt. 5:31-32; 19:4-10)
and the departure of an unbelieving spouse (1 Cor. 7:15),
death is God's only desired dissolution for marriage. Just as
the body of Christ is indivisible, God's ideal for marriage is
that it be indivisible. As Christ is one with His church, husbands are. one with their wives. Therefore a husband who
harms his wife harms himself, and a husband who violates
and destroys his marriage violates and destroys himself. And
if our society has taught us anything, it has taught us that.

Paul goes on to say, "This mystery is great; but I am speaking with reference to Christ and the church" (Eph. 5:32). Why is submission as well as sacrificial, purifying, and caring love so strongly emphasized in Scripture? Because the sacredness of the church is wed to the sacredness of marriage. Your marriage is either a symbol or a denial of Christ and His church.

The sacredness of marriage motivated Paul to conclude, "Let [the husband] love his own wife even as himself; and let the wife see to it that she respect her husband" (v. 33). There is no more definitive statement of God's ideal for marriage than that. When Christian husbands and wives walk in the power of the Spirit, yield to His Word and His control, and are mutually submissive, blessing is the result.

CHAPTER 4

The Excellent Wife
at Work

In recent years a mass of books have been published on feminism and the woman's liberation movement. One in particular, *A Lesser Life: The Myth of Women's Liberation in America* (New York: William Morrow and Co., 1986), written by economist Sylvia Ann Hewlett, who might be better described as a new feminist, essentially laments the lack of public and government support systems for working women. In her section titled "The Aberrant Fifties" she writes:

> In May 1983 I interviewed Faith Whittlesey at the White House. At that time she was assistant to the President for public liaison and dealt with policies toward women and children. I told her of my concern for working mothers in this country and explained in vivid detail how very hard it was for them to deal with childbirth and child care in the absence of family support policies. Whittlesey listened carefully and tried to respond. She told me that

Ronald Reagan was tremendously concerned about the care and nurturing of children and that he did in fact have a policy in this area. The policy was to lick inflation and encourage the economy to grow so that men could once more earn a family wage. A little puzzled, I asked her how she thought this would help. "Oh," said Whittlesey, smiling, "the rest is easy. Once men earn a family wage, all those women can go home and look after their own children in the way they did when I was growing up." Everything, it seems, would be solved if we returned to the good old days of the fifties, when moms were homemakers and dads were stalwart breadwinners (p. 231).

Whittlesey was right—although I doubt we will ever see our society or government ever embrace again what feminists, economists, and think-tank experts call an aberrant period in our nation's history.

To help her readers gain a better understanding of the '50s, Hewlett explained how this "aberrant" period came to be (pp. 231–52). Let's examine her account.

THE RISE AND FALL OF THE TRADITIONAL FAMILY

Throughout the second half of the nineteenth century, Europe envied the advances made by women in the United States. Even in the first third of the twentieth century, U.S. women made rapid strides. They acquired the vote earlier than women did in Britain, France, Italy, and Switzerland. Economic expansion and access to higher education offered women further opportunities for employment. Even divorce and contraception became widespread. By the end of the '30s, American women held a vast lead over their European counterparts.

As the Second World War broke out, a great need arose for women to take over the jobs American servicemen left behind. As a result, almost 5 million additional women entered the work force during that period. By 1945 American women were more powerful than ever before in our nation's history.

But something happened.

Our government faced a problem of monumental propor-
tions in 1945. After enduring ten years of a depression and
five more of a devastating war, Americans wanted a return to
normal life. But there was a great fear that jobs would be
scarce for the returning servicemen. So women were encouraged to return to their homes through a series of governmental and economic actions. Some were reactive: women were
laid off from jobs at double the rate of men and government-
sponsored child-care programs were shut down. But others
were proactive and had the most pronounced effect, such as
the GI Bill and the Highway Act. Hewlett explains the impact
of these two pieces of legislation:

> The GI Bill . . . provided 14 million returning veterans
> with free college tuition, subsistence allowances (which
> were increased by 50 percent if one had dependents),
> and extremely low-cost mortgages (guaranteed loans for
> thirty years at 3 to 4 percent interest); while the High-
> way Act of 1944 pumped $1.3 billion of public money
> into a road network around and between cities. . . .
>
> Through the GI Bill men . . . acquired a head start in
> the job market and were able to become good providers.
> It made little sense for couples to invest in the skills of a
> wife since she couldn't compete with all this free train-
> ing. Secondly, since dependents were at least partially
> supported through the provisions of the GI Bill, this
> legislation encouraged early marriage and procreation.
> Why not avail yourself of free income? Finally, the roads
> provided by the Highway Act and the cheap financing
> provided by the low-cost mortgages of the GI Bill ex-
> tended the possibility of living in a house in the suburbs
> to millions of young American couples (p. 243).

What was the result? Between 1945 and 1955 the American GNP more than doubled. Women got married at an earlier age. The birthrate rose so that by the end of the '50s the
rate of population growth was double that of Europe. Even
the divorce rate fell. Yet by the end of the decade, the Ameri-

can family was poised at the edge of cliff, ready to plunge in a freefall that has lasted over thirty years.

Fueled by an ever-increasing opportunity to acquire the good life, the '50s male breadwinner got caught up in the race to get ahead. But he wound up burned out from his job and isolated from his wife and children.

The '50s homemaker had to be the perfect wife, mother, and housekeeper. She was expected to have the sole responsibility of raising the children in an age of new permissive theories on how to do it, handed down from Freud to Spock. She also became enamored with the need to have a better lifestyle. So when her husband couldn't make enough to fund their materialistic dreams, she went to work.

As both men and women became more dissatisfied with their lot in life, feminism launched its attack on the family in the early '60s. Husbands and wives, frustrated by their lack of involvement in each other's lives, began to divorce in record numbers. Between 1965 and 1975 the divorce rate doubled. And children, victims of permissive child-rearing practices and seeing through the façade of their parents' empty pursuits, rebelled, turning to drugs and the counterculture to fill their emptiness.

Hewlett's assessment is sadly wrong. The family of the '50s failed not because women left the work force and what they had and could achieve to become homemakers (as feminists would have you believe); it failed because people are sinners who want to please themselves. You can't blame the traditional family for that. What went wrong with the American family? Why, when it had it so good, did it self-destruct? Is there something wrong with the biblical pattern for the family? The American family shattered for the simple reason it was American, not biblical. The '50s established a family arrangement that only happened to follow the biblical pattern, and actually was completely secular in its focus.

As we learned in the previous chapter, any family or society can benefit from biblical principles, and many did to such an extent that many who lived in those days long for a return to them. Ultimately though, only those who by faith in Christ have made Him the center of their families can realize the full and lasting power of those principles.

The need has never been more important as our society nears the midpoint of the '90s. The makeup of the family is far different than what it was thirty-five years ago. According to *Time,* "68% of women with children under 18 are in the work force (in contrast to 28% in 1960)" ("Onward Women," Dec. 4, 1989, 85). *Megatrends for Women* (Patricia Aburdene and John Naisbitt [New York: Fawcett Columbine, 1992], 238–39) reports that the traditional family with husband as breadwinner, homemaker wife, and children now accounts for only 10 percent of families. In 1970, 40 percent of households were married couples with children under eighteen. By 1991 that fell to 26 percent. Fifty-three percent of women with infants now work. By the year 2000 half of the work force will be women and more than 80 percent of women age twenty-five to fifty-four will work. If we give it enough time, no one will be home!

Christians, therefore, have a great opportunity to model the family ideal for our society in a day when people face so many options. The Apostle Paul was continually concerned that believers present a clear testimony to the pagan society, and in his epistle to Titus he focused on character qualities that should be true of believers in the church (2:1-10). We will be looking at that section in its entirety in a later chapter, but it is important that we examine one directive in particular: Paul's command to the older women to instruct the young women to be "workers at home" (v. 5).

HOME IS WHERE THE HEART IS

The phrase "workers at home" is translated from the compound Greek word *oikourgos,* which is derived from *oikos* (house) and a form of *ergon* (work). *Ergon* does not simply refer to labor in general; it often refers to a particular job or employment. It is the word Jesus used when He said, "My food is to do the will of Him who sent Me, and to accomplish His *work*" (John 4:34, emphasis added). Our Lord focused His entire life on fulfilling God's will. In a similar fashion, a wife is to focus her life on the home. God has designed the family to be her sphere of responsibility. That doesn't mean she should spend twenty-four hours a day there, however. The woman in Proverbs 31 left her home when she needed to buy a field or when she needed supplies, yet even those trips benefited her family. She poured her life into her family — she woke up early and went to bed late for the sake of those in it.

Notice that Paul didn't make any effort to elaborate on what he meant by "workers at home." That's because his readers were completely familiar with the term. The Mishna, an ancient codification of Jewish law and tradition, gives us some insight into what life was like for a wife in Paul's day. She was expected to grind flour, bake, launder, cook, nurse her children, make the beds, spin wool, prepare the children for school, and accompany them to school to ensure their arrival. While many women worked with their husbands in the field or in a trade, the husband still held the responsibility to provide food and clothing. If any women worked apart from their husbands in the marketplace or at a trade, they were considered a disgrace. A wife could, however, work at crafts or horticulture in the home and sell the fruits of her labor. Profits from her endeavors could then be used either to supplement her husband's income or provide her with some spending money. In addition to household work, wives were responsible for hospitality and the care of guests, and to be active in charitable work. The Jewish laws were clear: the woman's priority was in the home. She was to take care of all the needs of her home, her children, her husband, strangers, the poor and needy, and guests. The wife who faithfully discharged her responsibilities was held in high regard in her family, in the synagogue, and in the community.

That the New Testament required such a lifestyle for women is clear from the demands of 1 Timothy 5:9-10, 14: the wife of one man, having a reputation for good works, brought up children, shown hospitality to strangers, washed the saints' feet, assisted those in distress, devoted to every good work, kept house, and given the enemy no occasion for reproach.

Today we have many conveniences in the home that ancient people didn't have. We don't have to grind our own grain, make our own fabric, or go to a river to wash our clothes. That means keepers at home have more discretionary time now than before, so they need to be careful to use that time discreetly. There may be things they can do that will benefit the home, that will assist others, or that may even be enterprising like the Proverbs 31 woman and bring in some income. But the home is to remain the priority.

I certainly believe the value of this work has been severely underestimated over the years—mainly because of the feminist movement. One young husband and father who was obligated to serve a brief stint in caring for the home learned to appreciate his wife's responsibilities:

> I never realized how much work it takes to keep a house running. The first few weeks at home, I was amazed to find that shopping, cooking and cleaning up for three meals could take the whole day. But the household chores have been the easy part. The heavier burden—by far—has been entertaining, educating and disciplining my son. . . . "Quality time" is a myth. If I want a relationship with Derek, I have to put in the hours. If I don't, I miss out on my son's life. . . . One of the most demanding jobs in the world is also one of the most rewarding (Rholan Wong, "Full-Time Fatherhood: Hardest Job of All," *Los Angeles Times* [Sun. 6 Sept. 1992]:E6).

I can appreciate what that man is saying. When my wife broke her neck in a serious auto accident two years ago, I suddenly needed to do for her much of what she had been doing for me over the years. We didn't have any young children at home, so things were much easier than they could have been. Nevertheless, I was impressed—and almost overwhelmed sometimes—by the tremendous responsibilities of a diligent "worker at home."

It may surprise you, but the saying "A woman's place is in the home" has never sounded quite right to me. Rather, what the Bible is saying is *a woman's responsibility is in the home.* There's no virtue in just staying home; what's important is what you do when you're there. Just because a mother stays home doesn't mean she is spiritual. If she spends a hefty portion of her day watching soap operas or engaging in other profitless ventures, her influence could be as bad as that of a mother who works outside the home to the neglect of her children.

For a mother to get a job outside the home and put her children in day care is to misunderstand her husband's role as provider as well as her own duty to the family. Don't be tempted to work outside the home to pay for your children to go to a Christian school, for example. Better to stay in the home and raise your children to be godly rather than pass on that responsibility. The woman who raises a godly generation is making the greatest impact a woman can make on the world. No Christian school can ever match that. God has made clear through His Word that both parents have a great responsibility to pass on His truth to their children daily (Deut. 6:6-9; Prov. 6:20).

I realize that some mothers face difficulties that force them to work. In this age of economic insecurity, husbands are subject to layoffs and are unable to provide for their families for a period of time. There is also the tragedy of divorce and single mothers must become the provider. Unfortunately the greater majority of women choose to work outside the home for selfish reasons. Some have bought the lie that personal fulfillment comes from pursuing a career, not meeting the needs of their loved ones. Others work so they can earn extra income to increase their standard of living, and their husbands give hearty approval if not a downright mandate. To see mothers abandoning their three- and four-month-old babies to baby-sitters to do so flies in the face of God's design for wives and mothers.

If you cannot maintain a standard of living that allows you to fulfill your role consistent with God's design, you ought to reconsider carefully whether your standard is acceptable to God. It is better to learn to live with less, making whatever adjustments are necessary, such as renting a home instead of buying one. Don't presume that the economic benefits from having two incomes are God's blessing.

When women remove themselves from the sphere God has designed for them, they become subject to an environment fraught with difficulty. Two Christian women warn of a potential danger:

> Statistics show significantly more working women than stay-at-home moms become involved in extramarital affairs. . . . Why are we so vulnerable? One reason is simply *exposure*. . . . Another factor is *professional intimacy*. . . . Then there's *emotional need*. . . .
>
> If we are married to men who don't appreciate our professional interests or contributions, we may find ourselves attracted to the men at work who do. If we feel overwhelmed by the incredible responsibilities at home and at work, we may be all the more ready to exchange our grown-up burdens for the kind of romantic rush and blush we felt when we were 16. . . . Men and women in the workplace also invest the best hours of their day on the job. We're at our wittiest and our prettiest (Linda Holland and Karen Linamen, "Occupational Hazards," *Today's Christian Woman* [March–April 1991]:54–55).

Titus 2:5 says instead for wives to be "subject to their own husbands" (cf. Eph. 5:22). I'm concerned about women who get under powerful male-dominated environments because women can be easily abused. I'm therefore not surprised by the recent hue and cry of sexual harassment. Realistically speaking, most women at work are exposed to innuendo at best and sexual involvement at worst. The following warnings to Christian working women point up the problem:

> The best option simply is to avoid entanglements from the start. . . .
> - Arrange accountability to friends or to a spouse *before* a problem arises
> - Verbally practice saying "No" long before the opportunity arises
> - Avoid fantasies. . . .
> - Avoid frequent time alone with any male coworker

- Avoid intimate or "What if . . ." conversations with male friends
- Seek . . . help for obvious . . . "voids" in your marriage
- Maintain a vibrant relationship with God as well as consistent fellowship with other believers. Above all, recognize that *no one* is immune to an affair — so stay on guard ("Occupational Hazards," 56, emphasis in original).

God has designed women with a need for the protection that a godly husband and home provides. Men, it's up to us to take the lead in providing a haven for our wives, so that we are giving them the opportunity to provide a haven for us and for our children.

Certainly women with grown children or no children have a certain freedom in applying the "keepers at home" priority. But be selective and make wise decisions in what you choose to do outside the home so you won't compromise your priority to preserve your home as a haven for your husband and as a place of hospitality for others. I think it's especially wonderful when women choose to work in Christian ministry, such as teaching little ones in school, being involved in missions, or ministering to people in a jail or hospital setting. In pursuing ventures outside the home, go before the Lord and your husband, and decide jointly how to do only that which will enhance and enrich your home life and accomplish spiritual goals.

THE EXCELLENT WIFE

No other passage of Scripture gives us the model of the "worker at home" better than Proverbs 31. Here we see more than a wife in the role of a homemaker: we see her as the complete woman God designed her to be.

King Lemuel, the author of Proverbs 31, relates to us the wisdom he received from his mother on how to choose a wife. Verses 10-31 describe no specific woman, but they reveal the qualities and characteristics that every woman should seek to emulate.

The king writes, "An excellent wife, who can find? For her worth is far above jewels." The word translated "excellent" in the Hebrew text means "force" or "strength." Here it refers to the wife as a woman of strength — strong spiritually, morally, mentally, and physically. This woman makes a difference in society. And she is priceless: "Her worth is far above jewels" means she is more valuable than earthly things.

Typically men seek a wife for all the wrong reasons: looks, accomplishments, style, success, money, or education. They ought to look for a woman with virtue, strength of character, spiritual excellence, and internal godliness. Six specific qualities characterize the excellent wife.

Her Character as a Wife

King Lemuel relates her husband's perspective: "The heart of her husband trusts in her" (v. 11). This husband sees his wife as trustworthy, which allows him to work away from home, confident in her faithfulness, integrity, discretion, and care for all his interests. The context implies that she is responsible for a substantial home with abundant resources. Yet her husband is not at all anxious about leaving her with such a responsibility because he knows that his well-being is her concern, his comfort her passion, and his burdens hers to relieve.

As a result, "he will have no lack of gain" (v. 11) due to her careful stewardship. As both a wise and scrupulous ruler of the house, she manages the assets and coordinates all activities. Her ability to handle all domestic matters frees him to be devoted to his work.

On the personal side, "She does him good and not evil all the days of her life" (v. 12). With her husband's best interests at heart, she does everything she can to strengthen and encourage him. His money, possessions, and resources are safe with her. She never speaks evil of him or defames his character in public or in the privacy of their family. And that is her behavior "all the days of her life." Her love for him and devotion to the home don't fluctuate with the changing circumstances of life. When you got married you no doubt affirmed the vow to live together in sickness and in health, in joy and in sorrow, in plenty and in want, and that's a vow this woman kept for life. The purity and power of her devotion never changes. His comfort, success, reputation, and joy are always her delight.

The husband reaps the benefit of such faithfulness: "Her husband is known in the gates, when he sits among the elders of the land" (v. 23). That means he is esteemed and respected by his peers, in part because she created a world for him in which he could be everything God wanted him to be. Her life can best be described as selfless — her husband's good consumes her. That's why she loves to serve him.

Her Devotion as a Homemaker

The first specific characteristic of this enterprising woman's homemaking abilities is in verse 13: "She looks for wool and flax, and works with her hands in delight." Clothing her family is one of her first priorities. Looking for, rather than simply using, wool and flax means that she searched for quality products. Wool was used for making clothing for the colder seasons of the year; flax was used for linen, which was lighter and more appropriate for the warmer seasons. Flax was especially beneficial for making beautiful clothing. For her, making clothes for her husband and children was a joy.

Verse 14 describes the extent of her forays to find the right food for her family: "She is like merchant ships; she brings her food from afar." Continual trips to the local market for the standard fare was not her practice; she would travel distances to obtain the best food at the best price. She didn't just slap together whatever she had; she wanted to provide what she thought her family would enjoy. That required good planning and good management.

I'm not sure how much sleep this kind of woman gets, because verse 15 says, "She rises also while it is still night, and gives food to her household, and portions to her maidens." Typically people in those days would keep one small lamp burning through the night. Since the lamp held a small amount of oil, someone had to wake up during the night and add more oil to keep the lamp burning. This wife assumed that responsibility so her family could sleep. Then after filling the lamp, she didn't go back to bed; she stayed up to begin preparing the meals for that day! Once again we see her make a great sacrifice on behalf of her family.

The phrase "portions to her maidens" probably refers to portions of work, not food. This industrious wife not only began her own work at such an early hour but also apportioned different tasks to the maidens who were servants in the household. She demonstrates leadership.

Feminists and others who claim that the role of a homemaker is demeaning to women never understood Proverbs 31. A homemaker has to combine elements of an economist, administrator, and business manager to analyze available products, exercise wisdom and foresight to make intelligent purchases, and assign tasks to her household labor force. At the same time she has to fulfill her responsibilities as a wife to her husband and provide tender, loving care to all her children.

Beyond all those duties, the excellent wife is also an entrepreneur: "She considers a field and buys it; from her earnings she plants a vineyard" (v. 16). Her husband didn't give her the money to buy the field, she bought it and planted the vineyard with *her* earnings. Verse 24 describes the source of these earnings: "She makes linen garments and sells them, and supplies belts to the tradesmen." In addition to her family and household responsibilities, she earned extra money for herself by making and selling a useful product. Notice, however, that she did not mix her money with the household cash flow — she put it aside until the right opportunity came along.

Any woman who can fill all these roles must have tremendous energy: "She girds herself with strength, and makes her arms strong" (v. 17). "She girds herself with strength" could be translated "strength is wrapped around her." She is a strong woman in terms of self-discipline, commitment to her family, and love for her husband. "Her arms [are] strong" refers to her physical strength, which is a result of her daily labor.

Motivation is a key element in any task, and this woman was highly motivated. Verse 18 says, "She senses that her gain is good." Having bought the field and planted the vine-yard, she realized not just a financial profit, but spiritual blessing in seeing her family prosper from her labor. As a result, "her lamp does not go out at night" (v. 18). So fulfilled in seeing others benefit from her work, she is driven to work harder, even if it means staying awake all night to accomplish another task.

Perhaps it is on such nights that "she stretches out her hands to the distaff, and her hands grasp the spindle" (v. 19). Those are aspects of spinning, when she would actually turn the wool and the flax into thread. She may have had to make clothes for her family in the middle of the night because she was so busy during the day.

"She is not afraid of the snow for her household" (v. 21) means she was well-prepared for the winter, sewing well into the night to be sure her family had enough warm blankets for the night and warm clothes for the cold days. But she didn't settle just for functional clothes; she wanted her family to look good: "for all her household are clothed with scarlet" (v. 21). She actually dyed the wool to give it some beauty.

There is one respect in which this woman does think of herself: "She makes coverings for herself, her clothing is fine linen and purple" (v. 22). Grateful for the external beauty with which God has blessed her, she dresses in such a way that will show off her beauty to her husband. She doesn't overdo it with silk and gold and pearls. Instead she chooses linen, which wasn't a particularly expensive cloth. But we know it was the best she could make because of the care she took in choosing the best flax. And the beauty of the color purple would enhance her own beauty. Thus she avoids the extreme of ostentatious display by choosing graceful simplic-ity. That is characteristic of every decision she makes be-cause her goal is the well-being of her husband and children.

Her Generosity as a Neighbor

"She extends her hand to the poor; and she stretches out her hands to the needy" (v. 20). Based on what we've learned about this woman so far, we would expect nothing less. As devoted and loving as she is toward her own family, she does not neglect others. She demonstrates her compassion on the poor by becoming personally involved in their distress. She extends her hand—she touches them where they hurt, no doubt providing food and clothing.

The idea of extending her hand probably means that the poor approached her about their need, whereas stretching out her hands implies that she reached out to those who were too proud or embarrassed to express their need. While she may be focused on her family, she is not myopic.

Her Influence as a Teacher

Teaching begins with character: "Strength and dignity are her clothing, and she smiles at the future" (v. 25). "Strength" describes her spiritual character, while "dignity" defines the quality of her life. Both are foundational to her integrity as a teacher. She is truly spiritual—if she wasn't, her children wouldn't listen to her or obey her instruction. It is imperative for those who teach to live out what they teach, otherwise they are just purveyors of hypocrisy.

The fact that "she smiles at the future" means she doesn't fear it because she knows all things are in God's hands. We've seen how well-prepared she is: All will be well in the future for her because she's right with God. All be well in the future for her household because she has kept it in order. All will be well in the future for her children because she has been consistently raising them "in the discipline and instruction of the Lord" (Eph. 6:4). And all will be well in the future for her husband because her commitment to manage the home has given him the opportunity to be a man of God.

After character comes instruction: "She opens her mouth in wisdom" (Prov. 31:26). Scripture calls the father to be the teacher, the family priest, in the home. But that does not preclude the reality that the mother will daily apply the truth of life to her children. Proverbs 6:20 says, "Do not forsake the teaching of your mother."

Her dominant attitude when she teaches is loving-kindness: "The teaching of kindness is on her tongue" (Prov. 31:26). With gracious and kind words, she edifies and ministers grace to her hearers (Eph. 4:29).

Her Effectiveness as a Mother

Proverbs 31:27 sums up her leadership in the house: "She looks well to the ways of her household, and does not eat the bread of idleness." In exercising constant and excellent surveillance over the entire household, she never succumbs to the temptations of laziness. Instead she realizes that true fulfillment can only come from a supreme effort.

The old saying is true: What goes around comes around. If you mothers will invest your lives in your children in the first half of your life, you'll reap the dividends in the second half. The excellent wife and mother raises her children with godly wisdom and great love and care. Once her children are old enough to be on their own, they will spend the remainder of their years blessing the woman who gave up her life for them. That's God's design. The compensation for old age is the devotion of one's children. You receive the return on your investment through the blessing your children are to you when they are adults.

There's another benefit: When your children become parents, they'll follow your pattern in raising their children. That's why tender guidance, wise counsel, loving discipline, holy example, hard work, and unselfish giving are such vital characteristics in parenting. They'll provide constant guidance to your children as they try to emulate them before their own children.

There is one more dividend yet for the excellent wife: "Her husband [blesses her], and he praises her, saying, 'Many daughters have done nobly, but you excel them all'" (vv. 28-29). When a husband tells his wife that she's the best of all women, that's her ultimate reward.

Her Excellence as a Person

Her excellence as a person starts with the spiritual dimension, but first comes a warning: "Charm is deceitful" (v. 30). That refers to bodily form, and that is deceitful. Women who spend hours trying to improve their external looks miss out on what has lasting value: "A woman who fears the Lord, she shall be praised. Give her the product of her hands, and let her works praise her in the gates" (vv. 30-31). King Lemuel's mother's ideal for the excellent wife is wrapped up in those two verses. When a man can share his life with a woman who fears and loves God, he's in the best of circumstances. And if he thinks she is beautiful at first, she'll become more beautiful to him with every passing year.

Catharine Beecher was the oldest child of a famous family in American history. One of her younger sisters was novelist Harriet Beecher Stowe, author of *Uncle Tom's Cabin.* Both grew up having a great love for children, finding joy in the duties of raising and caring for them. At the age of twenty-three Catharine founded The Hartford Female Seminary. Its purpose was to train women to be lovers of their husbands and children, and keepers of the home. She and Harriet founded another seminary a few years later in Cincinnati, Ohio. In 1869 they wrote a book entitled *The American Woman's Home* (New York: J.B. Ford and Co.). In it they stated,

> Woman's profession embraces the care and nursing of the body in the critical periods of infancy and sickness, the training of the human mind in the most impressionable period of childhood . . . and most of the government and economies of the family state. These duties of woman are as sacred and important as any ordained to man; and yet no such advantages for preparation have been accorded her, nor is there any qualified body to certify the public that a woman is duly prepared to give proper instruction in her profession (p. 14).

It was their desire in founding the two schools to train women "not only to perform in the most approved manner all the manual employments of domestic life, but to honor and enjoy these duties" (pp. 14–15). That noble work is not emphasized or appreciated anywhere near to the degree it should be. That will turn around when single and married men and women embrace instead of chafe against God's ideal of young women being "workers at home" (Titus 2:5), joyfully making whatever sacrifices are necessary at the appropriate time in their lives, encouraging others to do the same.

CHAPTER 5

A Different Place in God's Plan

Simple math states the obvious: if 26 percent of all households in the United States are made up of married couples, that means 74 percent must incorporate those who are divorced, widowed, and single. Certainly those percentages would change when applied to the church, which upholds the sanctity of marriage to a far greater degree than secular society. But when we figure in those believers who are married to unbelievers, many people in the church don't match the ideal for marriage we examined in the previous chapters.

In this chapter we will see God's design for those who are married to unbelievers, a widow or divorced woman, or single. His will for their lives is rich and fulfilling.

IF YOU ARE MARRIED TO AN UNBELIEVER
The Lord is not discriminatory when He chooses people for His kingdom — they come from all situations. It is not surprising, therefore, to see only one spouse out of a marriage rela-

tionship come to Christ. Just as we do today, the church in the first century had to teach new believers how to treat their unsaved spouses. Husbands wanted to know if they should continue to treat their wives in the dominant manner characteristic of the secular society. Wives wanted to know if they should reject the authority of their non-Christian husbands in favor of their new allegiance to a higher authority, who is Christ. Should their new status in Christ require that they demand their physical and spiritual rights? Both the Apostle Paul (1 Cor. 7:12-16) and the Apostle Peter (1 Peter 3:1-7) offer timeless and specific guidelines that believers should follow when married to an unbeliever.

What You Shouldn't Do
The natural, human tendency for many married to non-Christians, and in particular a wife in that society, would be to abandon the relationship. The Christian perspective, however, is just the opposite. Paul counsels,

> If any brother has a wife who is an unbeliever, and she consents to live with him, let him not send her away. And a woman who has an unbelieving husband, and he consents to live with her, let her not send her husband away. For the unbelieving husband is sanctified through his wife, and the unbelieving wife is sanctified through her believing husband; for otherwise your children are unclean, but now they are holy (1 Cor. 7:12-14).

The phrase "send away" as used in the context of man–woman relationships means divorce. Paul had previously counseled married believers not to divorce because Christ had forbidden it (vv. 10-11). Here he counsels those believers who were unequally yoked not to divorce a spouse if he or she agreed to maintain the relationship. There are several advantages in preserving the marriage.

Being unequally yoked can be frustrating, discouraging, and even costly. But it need not be defiling because rather than the believer being corrupted by the unbeliever, the believer can sanctify a home. In this sense sanctify does not refer to salvation; it refers to being set apart for goodness from God. All the blessings and grace of God that accrue to that one believer will spill over and enrich the unsaved spouse and other family members.

In addition, although the believer's faith cannot accomplish salvation for anyone but himself, the power of his or her testimony is often the means by which other family members come to faith in Christ.

Furthermore, God regards the family as a unit. Even if it is divided spiritually, and most of its members are unbelieving and immoral, God graces the entire family through the believer among them. Therefore, if your unbelieving spouse is willing to stay, don't seek a divorce. He or she is better off in a place where God is granting a blessing.

If an unbelieving partner does not consent to live with a Christian, however, Paul offers the following instruction: "If the unbelieving [spouse] leaves, let him leave; the brother or sister is not under bondage in such cases, but God has called us to peace. For how do you know, O wife, whether you will save your husband? Or how do you know, O husband, whether you will save your wife?" (vv. 15-16) It's simple: if your husband or wife wants out, let him or her go.

In God's sight the bond between a husband and wife is dissolved only by death (Rom. 7:2), adultery (Matt. 19:9), and the desertion of an unbelieving spouse. When the bond is broken in any of those ways, a Christian is free to remarry. By implication, the permission given to a widow or widower to remarry (Rom. 7:3) can extend to the present case, where a believer is no longer bound.

God allows divorce in this case because He "has called us to peace" (1 Cor. 7:15). If your wife or husband can't tolerate your faith and wants out of the marriage, it is better to dissolve your marriage to preserve your peace. Fighting, turmoil, bickering, criticism, and frustration disrupt the harmony and peace God desires for His children. And don't use evangelism as a just cause for maintaining a marriage if the spouse wants to leave; you have no guarantee of leading your spouse to Christ in an uncomfortable, chaotic, and confused environment.

Let me add one caution: don't let overbearing Gospel presentations be the source of your spouse's desire to leave the relationship. You cannot badger a person into the kingdom. Live the kind of life that will draw your spouse to Christ instead of driving him or her away.

What Wives Can Do

Becoming a Christian can pose some serious problems today just as it did 2,000 years ago. As we've noted, women were treated with little respect in the Greek and Roman culture of Paul's day. As long as they lived in their father's house, they were under the Roman law of *patria potestas* (the father's power), which gave fathers the power of life and death over their daughters. Once a woman married, her husband had the same legal power. Since it was socially taboo for women to make their own decisions, a decision on their part to follow Christ sometimes resulted in severe abuse from their unbelieving husbands. In spite of such difficult circumstances, the believing wife could win her husband to Christ by fulfilling certain responsibilities.

Be Submissive

Peter says, "In the same way, you wives, be submissive to your own husbands so that even if any of them are disobedient to the word, they may be won without a word by the behavior of their wives" (1 Peter 3:1). A wife is just as obligated to submit to her husband whether he is a Christian or not. "In the same way" refers back to the submission of citizens to civil authorities (2:13) and employees to their employers (v. 18). As we learned in chapter 2, God ordains such an arrangement for the smooth operation of all social institutions, including marriage.

"Disobedient to the word" describes the husband who rejects the Gospel. That phrase is a first-class conditional in the Greek text, which means that it's a reality. It could be translated "since they are disobedient to the Word." A believing wife should submit to her husband so he might be won to Christ "without a word." That doesn't refer to *the* Word of God, since that is essential for anyone's salvation (1:23), but to spoken words. A wife wins her husband to Christ not by what she says, but how she behaves. That doesn't mean she shouldn't communicate the Gospel to him, but her lovely, gracious, gentle, submissive attitude is her most effective evangelistic tool.

Be Faithful

Husbands will be won to Christ "as they observe [their] chaste and respectful behavior" (3:2). Wives need to live pure lives, characterized by irreproachable conduct and faithfulness both to God and to their husbands. Don't allow yourself to become involved with another man; instead be respectful to your husband.

Be Modest

Wives, especially in our society, need to take heed to Peter's warning in verse 3: "Let not your adornment be merely external — braiding the hair, and wearing gold jewelry, or putting on dresses." In Roman society women were continually preoccupied with their external appearance. They dyed their hair outlandish colors, braided it elaborately, and were fond of expensive jewelry, elegant clothing, and fine cosmetics. Certainly Peter wasn't forbidding women from styling their hair or wearing jewelry and nice clothing; he just didn't want them to be preoccupied with those things.

Ladies, external beauty will never capture your husband's heart if it's not backed by a beautiful attitude. Your primary focus should be on "the hidden person of the heart, with the imperishable quality of a gentle and quiet spirit" (v. 4). A humble, calm disposition characterizes inner beauty, and "is precious in the sight of God" (v. 4). Pursue virtue and you'll stand a much better chance of winning your husband to Christ.

Although God highly values the inner beauty of godliness, that's no excuse for sloppiness. Underdoing it will draw as much attention to your outward appearance as overdoing it. You've dressed appropriately when your outward appearance simply reflects the inner beauty God has fashioned within you.

Verses 5-6 illustrate what inner beauty is all about: "In this way in former times the holy women also, who hoped in God, used to adorn themselves, being submissive to their own husbands. Thus Sarah obeyed Abraham, calling him lord, and you have become her children if you do what is right without being frightened by any fear." "Holy women" refers to Old Testament women believers. Verse 6 specifically names Sarah as the model of submission because of her obvious respect for her husband, Abraham. All true believers are children of Abraham by faith (Rom. 4:5-16; Gal. 3:7-29), and likewise all believing women who follow Sarah's example are her spiritual progeny.

The absence of much literature by evangelical feminists on this verse is telling. It is very difficult, if not impossible, to dispute the biblical principle of authority and submission. J. David Pawson writes, "Peter's language goes somewhat further than Paul's; he commends Sarah for calling Abraham 'Lord' . . . and giving him the obedience due to someone deserving that title" *(Leadership Is Male* [Nashville: Thomas Nelson, 1990], 63).

"Without being frightened by any fear" (1 Peter 3:6) speaks of intimidation. It seems every society since the Fall has tried to intimidate wives into not submitting to their husbands. But instead of being intimidated, the wife is to "do what is right" by being submissive, tactful, modest, and gentle.

What Husbands Should Do

First Peter 3:7 says, "You husbands likewise, live with your wives in an understanding way, as with a weaker vessel, since she is a woman; and grant her honor as a fellow heir of the grace of life, so that your prayers may not be hindered." Husbands, if you want to win your wives to Christ, be faithful to do the following:

Be Considerate

"Understanding" speaks of being sensitive to your wife's deepest physical and emotional needs. In other words, be thoughtful and respectful. Remember, you are to nourish and cherish her (Eph. 5:25-28). Many women have said to me, "My husband doesn't understand me. We never talk. He doesn't know how I feel or what I'm thinking about." Such insensitivity builds walls in marriages. "Live with your wives in an understanding way" is another way of saying, "Be considerate." It isn't what you get out of marriage but what you put into it that brings glory to God. Do you know your wife's needs? Have you discussed them with her? Have you asked her what kind of husband she wants you to be?

Be Chivalrous

By God's design, a wife is to be the special object of her husband's love and care. As "a weaker vessel" she is under his authority and protection. "Weaker" doesn't mean weaker spiritually or intellectually, but physically and perhaps emotionally. Scripture indicates that in several places. For example, in Jeremiah 51:30 we read, "The mighty men of Babylon have ceased fighting, they stay in the strongholds; their strength is exhausted, they are becoming like women; their dwelling places are set on fire, the bars of her gates are broken" (cf. Isa. 19:16; Jer. 50:37; Nahum 3:13). Babylon's army was compared to women because it was afraid, without strength, and defenseless.

It's not a negative thing for a woman to be a weaker vessel. In making the man stronger, God designed a wonderful partnership. One way a husband can protect and provide for his wife is to practice chivalry. Whatever happened to the custom of opening the car door for your wife? Some husbands are fifteen feet down the driveway while the wife still has one foot out the door! Look for ways to be courteous that you know she will appreciate.

Be a Companion

"Grant her honor" is another way of saying, "Treat your wife with respect" while "grace of life" is a reference to marriage. "Grace" simply means "a gift," and one of the best gifts life has to offer is marriage. Thus when Peter says to give her respect as a "fellow heir of the grace of life," he is commanding husbands to respect their wives as equal partners in the marriage. Another way to win her to Christ is to cultivate companionship and friendship. That necessitates sharing your life with her and developing mutual interests. Think about things you can do together. One of the secrets of a happy relationship is finding commonality.

These aren't mere casual suggestions. According to Peter, your applying them has a direct bearing on how your prayers are answered. Since those prayers would include petitions for her salvation, don't neglect being considerate, chivalrous, and a companion to your unsaved wife.

IF YOU ARE A WIDOW OR DIVORCED WOMAN

Among the neediest people in our society are those women who are either widowed or divorced, and the Apostle Paul provides instructions to married and single men and women in the church on how to care for them. He says, "Honor widows who are widows indeed" (1 Tim. 5:3).

The Greek term translated "widows" means "bereft" and conveys a sense of suffering loss or being left alone. It does not tell us how a woman became a widow, so the cause is not limited to a husband's death. *A widow in the biblical sense may be a daughter, a mother, a sister, a niece, or an aunt who loses her husband through divorce, desertion, imprisonment, or especially death.* Caring for such a woman is a privilege and a manifestation of God's compassion.

More and more women in our society are in need of such compassion. George Grant, in his book *The Dispossessed: Homelessness in America,* details how detrimental the feminist movement has been to the well-being of women ([Westchester, Ill.: Crossway, 1986], 73–79). He uses the phrase "the feminization of poverty" to describe its negative effect: "It has broken down traditional family structures. It has contributed to epidemic irresponsibility. It has diminished courtesy, respect, and commitment. It has opened a Pandora's box of social ills, not the least of which is the progressive impoverishment of the very women it was supposed to liberate" (p. 73).

Grant cites Lenore J. Weitzman, who notes in her book *The Divorce Revolution* that women experience a significant decline in their standard of living after a divorce, while their former husbands' standard of living increases. He also cites Kim Hopper and Jill Hamberg, who report in their book *The Making of America's Homeless* that one in three families with women as the head of the household is poor, compared with one in ten in those led by men, and one in nineteen where the home has two parents.

Maggie Gallagher spells out what these statistics mean:

> Women are more likely to be abandoned by their husbands, to have to raise their children alone, to slip into poverty and to experience all the consequent degradations, to live in crowded apartments in dangerous parts of the city, to experience bad health and poor medical care, to be beaten, stabbed, raped, and robbed. . . . Reversing historic trends, women today work longer and harder than their mothers did and, under the stress, are more likely to collapse in nervous breakdowns. Fewer women can find suitable marriage partners and many who do marry will never have the children for which they long *(Enemies of Eros* [Chicago: Bonus, 1989], 14).

Those tragic trends are far from God's ideal. By His design, a wife is to be the special object of her husband's love and care. But if a woman loses her husband, she is often left without any means of financial support. Such women are under God's special care. The Book of James summarizes God's compassion for widows: "This is pure and undefiled religion in the sight of our God and Father, to visit . . . widows in their distress" (1:27).

Paul wanted the entire church to demonstrate its faith that way. His discourse on widows (1 Tim. 5:3-16) gives several practical principles. Verse 3 states, "Honor widows who are widows indeed." Christian widows left alone are to receive financial support from the church if they meet the qualifications. "Honor" is a reference to the fifth commandment about honoring one's parents (Ex. 20:12), which the Jewish people since the days of Moses have understood to include financial aid (cf. Matt. 15:1-6).

Evaluating Needs

"Widows indeed" are distinguished from widows having financial means. Some husbands may have left their wives with wonderful resources such as a home and adequate funds. In those instances, the church should provide for any spiritual needs and come alongside with encouragement, love, and support in every way possible.

We live in a country that provides some basic coverage for widows, but as we have seen, the scope of their needs — and the number of needy women who could be classified in their ranks — is increasing dramatically. Some widows might desire a Christian education for their children, and the church could set up a scholarship fund toward meeting that need. Some of them may have previously survived on a low income while others may have benefited from a much higher one. The church needs to be wise in determining which needs are pressing.

That is a major commitment. It may even require transferring money out of other church programs at times. Obviously, then, the church cannot indiscriminately give to everyone, so Scripture establishes guidelines to determine who qualifies and who doesn't.

When Family Is Available

First Timothy 5:4 says, "If any widow has children or grandchildren, let them first learn to practice piety in regard to their own family, and to make some return to their parents; for this is acceptable in the sight of God." Family members have the primary responsibility of caring for widows. An essential way of demonstrating godliness in the context of family living is making sure each member is provided for. Verse 8 says, "If anyone does not provide for his own, and especially for those of his household, he has denied the faith, and is worse than an unbeliever."

Notice this responsibility doesn't apply only to older family members but to children *and* grandchildren. That's appropriate since godly young people will desire good relationships with their family members, for that is an indicator of true spirituality.

The basic principle, then, is for children to "make some return" on the investment their parents made in their lives, which includes a financial obligation. Children, don't ever take for granted the love and encouragement your parents gave you in addition to the basic material needs they provided such as food, clothing, and housing.

When Family Isn't Available
Some family members don't always see things from the divine perspective, however. Verse 5 acknowledges that some are widows "indeed," defined as those who have "been left alone." They don't have any children or grandchildren who are willing to care for them either because of immorality, divorce, abandonment by the children, or even the children's deaths.

The church's first criterion for supporting a widow is when she has no one to turn to for help, and the second is this: That she "has fixed her hope on God, and continues in entreaties and prayers night and day" (v. 5). That describes a mature Christian. Her prayer life is reflective of an intimate relationship with the Lord. That is quite a contrast to the widow described in verse 6: "But she who gives herself to wanton pleasure is dead even while she lives." This woman, who is alive physically but dead spiritually, lives with disregard for what is right and without devotion to God. The implication is she should be left to the consequences of her sins, which hopefully will lead her to repent. The church is not responsible to help widows like that, especially those who continue a sinful lifestyle.

A situation almost as bad as that is this: "If anyone does not provide for his own, and especially for those of his household, he has denied the faith, and is worse than an unbeliever" (v. 8). "Provide" means "to think of beforehand" or "to care for," indicating that support requires careful forethought and planning. "His own" is a general reference to the believer's sphere of relationships—friends, neighbors, acquaintances, and especially relatives. "Any" indicates *every believer is responsible to support the needy.* When he or she can, a believer should meet needs without taking it to the organized church. The believer who doesn't is guilty of withholding love and setting a poor example.

Most unbelievers take care of their own because it's natural for them to do so (Matt. 7:9-11). When a believer doesn't fulfill an obligation that even an unbeliever knows enough to do, he is acting worse than an unbeliever. Even pagans revere their elders and ancestors.

Maintaining a High Standard

Christians have a higher standard, one that is reflected in these qualifications of godly widows who served the church in an official capacity:

> Let a widow be put on the list only if she is not less than sixty years old, having been the wife of one man, having a reputation for good works, and if she has brought up children, if she has shown hospitality to strangers, if she has washed the saints' feet, if she has assisted those in distress, and if she has devoted herself to every good work (1 Tim. 5:9-10).

Here the emphasis switches from financial support to qualifications for official status. We know the early church had elders and both men and women deacons (3:1-13). Apparently a group of godly widows were also considered church workers.

Their service included teaching and counseling the church's younger women, visiting the sick, and providing hospitality to travelers such as itinerant preachers. They had a ministry to children as well. In Paul's day, many unwanted children were abandoned in the marketplace. From this pool boys were trained as gladiators and girls were trained as prostitutes. The church widows sought out such abandoned children and placed them in good homes so they could receive proper care. If today's church had a group of godly widows with the same occupation, countless needy children would benefit.

A Mature Woman

The first qualification Paul listed for church widows is that they be at least sixty years old (5:9). In many cultures it is common to associate that age with maturity. Remember, however, this age limit is associated with her qualification as a church worker, not for receiving financial support (for which need, not age, is the main consideration).

A Devoted Wife

"Having been the wife of one man" (v. 9) is literally translated "a one-man woman." Paul wasn't referring to a woman who was married only once because he says in verse 14 that it is best if younger widows remarry and that a widow may "be married to whom she wishes, only in the Lord" (1 Cor. 7:39). Rather, he was emphasizing the devotion she showed to her husband when he was still alive. She was known to be faithful to him, and their marriage had no blemishes.

A Devoted Mother

"She has brought up children" (1 Tim. 5:10) implies her children benefited spiritually from her godly influence. They received nourishment in a spiritual environment. Being a mother is one of the greatest privileges a woman can have because of her effect on her children's character. That doesn't mean a woman without children is less valuable to God. But bringing up children is the norm for most women, and the mother who continues in "faith and love and sanctity with self-restraint" (2:15) is a model that other women should imitate.

Hospitable

"She has shown hospitality to strangers" (5:10) refers mainly to housing missionaries, evangelists, and other Christians who traveled often. Many times they were seeking refuge from persecutors, so this was a vital ministry. The Bible's commendation of Phoebe as "a helper of many" probably included, among other things, her aid to traveling saints (Rom. 16:1-2).

Humble

"She has washed the saints' feet" (1 Tim. 5:10) refers to a menial task often given to slaves. In ancient times, all the roads were either dusty or muddy, so it was a common courtesy to provide footwashing for visitors. In Christian circles, washing someone's feet came to symbolize humility (John 13:15). When they see a person in need, godly women should do what they can to help that person, no matter how lowly the task. Be prepared: Service that pleases Christ is often done at personal inconvenience and not for personal profit.

Unselfish
"She has assisted those in distress" (1 Tim. 5:10) speaks of those under pressure, whether mental, physical, or emotional. The word translated "assisted" appears only here and in verse 16. Its use in verse 16 indicates support, which might include money, meals, housing, or counsel to ease others' burdens. Her time is spent on others, not herself.

Kind
"She has devoted herself to every good work" (v. 10) reminds me of Dorcas, who made clothes for widows. Widows wept when they thought they had lost one who cared so much (Acts 9:39). Likewise, the widow described here is one who helps others and is kind.

Encouraging Remarriage Where Appropriate
Older widows free from the duties of caring for a spouse and children can devote time and effort to a variety of fruitful ministries. The church should heartily encourage them to do so, especially for the sake of the needy women and children they could assist. But the church is to give different advice to younger widows:

> Refuse to put younger widows on the list, for when they feel sensual desires . . . they want to get married, thus incurring condemnation, because they have set aside their previous pledge. And at the same time they also learn to be idle . . . and . . . also gossips and busybodies. . . . Therefore, [encourage] younger widows to get married, bear children, keep house, and give the enemy no occasion for reproach (1 Tim. 5:11-14).

Picture a young woman, widowed through divorce perhaps, who is feeling hurt and brokenhearted. In the emotion of the moment she says to the church, "I'll never marry again. I pledge to devote the rest of my life to serving the Lord. Please place me on your staff so I can minister with other women." Since it is difficult to sustain a commitment made during a time of grief, the church is to refuse any such request.

To Avoid Frustration

There are even more practical reasons for refusing the request. The first is that it's natural and beneficial for a young widow to desire to remarry after her initial grief. Since she was married before, the odds are she doesn't have the gift of singleness. That's especially true if she has young children to care for. Since "it's better to marry than to burn" (1 Cor. 7:9), no young widow should be made to feel that marriage is an unspiritual option. If a woman did feel that way, she would become frustrated, and that could lead to anger against the Lord.

In the context of ministry, a younger widow going from home to home, instructing and counseling other church women, could collect a lot of information about their personal lives. But if out of resentment she no longer wanted to serve others, she would be in a position to cause much damage.

To Find Fulfillment

As we have seen consistently from God's Word, the way most young women find fulfillment is to "get married, bear children, [and] keep house" (1 Tim. 5:14). By recommending that course of action, the church is giving "the enemy no occasion for reproach." The needs of younger women and children will be better met, older women will be more available for a variety of ministries and less likely to be obliged to provide primary care for a working mother's children, and younger and older men will have the satisfaction of helping society's neediest members in a truly effective way.

The church's instruction reflects our Lord's compassion in caring for widows. That doesn't mean every young woman who loses her husband and doesn't remarry will cause trouble or become a gossip. Obviously there are exceptions, as 1 Corinthians 7 teaches. But a godly husband can give a bereft widow the affection and care she needs.

Adding a Woman's Touch

To provide balance, Paul concludes: "If any woman who is a believer has dependent widows, let her assist them, and let not the church be burdened, so that it may assist those who are widows indeed" (1 Tim. 5:16). Christian women of means should support any widows in their fold to free up the church's funds as much as possible. Some of those women might be widows themselves. Their support doesn't always have to be money—it could be meals, lodging, or clothing.

Caring for women in need ought to be a joy for us because it's our Lord's joy. When the widow who is in your midst can "come and eat and be satisfied," the Lord your God will bless you in all the work that you do (Deut. 14:29).

IF YOU ARE SINGLE

In spite of how blessed marriage can be, God wants you to know *life can be just as rich whether you're married or not.* That's His message in select portions of 1 Corinthians 7. Here the Apostle Paul presents a counterbalance to the truth that marriage is "the grace of life": If you get married, you are going to have "trouble in this life" (v. 28). The word Paul used is alternately translated "tribulation" in the New Testament. In addition, your interests will be divided (vv. 32-35). Is marriage really a bad thing then? Of course not. Let's explore the balanced perspective Paul presents to gain a better understanding.

Celebrating Singleness

In verse 1 Paul begins, "It is good for a man not to touch a woman." "To touch a woman" was a common Jewish euphemism for sexual intercourse. Paul is saying it is good not to be involved in a sexual relationship—that it is good to be single. That is an important affirmation, especially since people in society and even the church can be insensitive, condescending, and rude toward those who are single by assuming something is wrong with them or they are desperate to get married.

Single life was even worse in Paul's day. Unbiblical Jewish teaching asserted that if you didn't have a wife, you were a sinner. According to the rabbis, there were seven kinds of people who couldn't get to heaven, and number one was a Jew who had no wife. The second was a wife who had no children. They theorized that since God said be fruitful and multiply (Gen. 1:28), you were being disobedient if you remained single.

God did declare at creation that "it is not good for the man to be alone; I will make him a helper suitable for him" (2:18). It is true that all people need companionship, but you can be single and not be alone. You can have friends, and God will bring people into your life to fulfill your need for companionship. Singleness before Him is a good, honorable, and excellent state.

The Difficulty of Being Single
Singleness is not without problems, however, which is why Paul says, "Because of immoralities, let each man have his own wife, and let each woman have her own husband" (1 Cor. 7:2). Because unfulfilled sexual desire can be very strong, those who are not married can suffer great temptation, especially in societies such as ours where sexual freedom is freely practiced and even glorified.

No sin that a person commits has more built-in pitfalls than sexual sin. It has broken more marriages, shattered more homes, caused more heartache and disease, and destroyed more lives than drugs and alcohol combined. That is why in the New Testament we read, "This is the will of God, your sanctification; that is, that you abstain from sexual immorality; that each of you know how to possess his own vessel in sanctification and honor" (1 Thes. 4:3-4). Every believer is to keep his or her own body under control.

In speaking about the danger of celibacy, Paul is not downgrading the institution of marriage by suggesting that marriage is God's escape valve for the sex drive. He is saying, however, that it is normal to get married because it is normal to have physical desire.

The Gift of Singleness
To clarify his position Paul says,

> I wish that all men were even as I myself am. However, each man has his own gift from God, one in this manner, and another in that. But I say to the unmarried and to widows that it is good for them if they remain even as I. But if they do not have self-control, let them marry; for it is better to marry than to burn (1 Cor. 7:7-9).

Some Christians aren't married because they have a special gift of God and are uniquely prepared by the Holy Spirit for singleness. People who have the gift of celibacy enjoy being single and are not tempted to fall into sexual sin or become preoccupied with marriage. When the rare exception arises, they are able to control it quickly. Jesus alluded to the gift when He said, "There are eunuchs who were born that way from their mother's womb; and there are eunuchs who were made eunuchs by men; and there are also eunuchs who made themselves eunuchs for the sake of the kingdom of heaven" (Matt. 19:12). The last group of single persons Jesus mentioned decided not to marry so they could fully serve the Lord and His kingdom. First Corinthians 7 clarifies that the ability to make that decision is a gift from the Holy Spirit.

Many pressures face single people in today's society, especially when considering the current emphasis on marriage and the family. It has been said that loneliness for single people is at its height during the holiday season, especially for single parents. But you don't have to feel that way. If God has given you the gift of singleness, accept that as His plan. Since He is a loving and all-wise God, He has your best interests at heart.

What If You Don't Think You Have the Gift?
In 1 Corinthians 7:8 Paul addresses the "unmarried" (a term best understood in this context to refer to divorced individ-

uals) and widows. In saying, "It is good for them if they remain even as I," he identifies with them rather than with "virgins" (v. 25, individuals who have never been married). It is likely Paul was a widower. In verse 9 he admits that whether previously married or not, it can be too difficult for some people to remain single: "If they do not have self-control, let them marry; for it is better to marry than to burn."

Those who believe they don't have the gift of singleness can become frustrated when they can't seem to find a marriage partner. If you're in that situation, don't be preoccupied with your predicament but with the Lord's kingdom. Here's why: *The best way to find the right person is to be the right person.* If you are living a righteous life and you do not have the gift of singleness, rest assured that God will provide a partner for you. How could He want you to be married, and yet not provide a partner?

Once you find the right person and decide to get married, be sure to do it fairly soon because of the temptation you'll face. As Paul said, "It is better to marry than to burn." Marriage was designed to help you be fulfilled sexually. The practical problems of an early marriage are not nearly as serious as the danger of immorality. I'm not advocating that you jump into marriage to gratify your sexual desire, but realize there is no advantage to long engagements.

Here are some practical ideas single people, whether gifted with singleness or not, can do to control their sexual desires.

Control What Goes into Your Mind
Your thinking controls your emotions and behavior (cf. Prov. 23:7). Instead of exposing yourself to music, movies, books, television programs, and advertisements with implicit or explicit references to immoral behavior and attitudes, fill your mind with divine truth by being a devoted student of Scripture.

Avoid Enticing Situations
The Bible doesn't tell us to stand our ground and fight sexual temptation, but to flee (1 Cor. 6:18; 2 Tim. 2:22).

Be Accountable to a Close Christian Friend
It may be best for you to avoid living or traveling alone.
Regularly and honestly confide in someone who is trustwor-
thy, mature, and understanding.

Be Content
Recognize that, for now, God has chosen for you to live without sex. And, He has promised not to allow any temptation in
your life that is too strong for you to handle (1 Cor. 10:13).
Knowing that will help you say with Paul, "I have learned to
be content in whatever circumstances I am" (Phil. 4:11).

Seek Love, Not Marriage
Show Christlike love to all your Christian brothers and sisters, and let God bring about a marriage if it is His will.
People who make marriage their goal often wind up marrying
the wrong person. Don't be preoccupied with finding the
right person. Instead, work on becoming the person God
wants you to be. Know that God will, in His time, lead you to
the person He has chosen for you.

The Advantages of Being Single
A great deal of contemporary literature and programs for
singles are directed toward helping them "endure" while
they wait for marriage. They seem to reflect an underlying
assumption that singleness isn't quite normal and certainly
not desirable. Instead of panicking if their son or daughter
hasn't married by a certain age, godly parents will consider
whether God has designed their child to be single. First
Corinthians 7:25-40 is a ready reference for them and the
rest of us. There Paul writes about the many advantages of
being single.

Less Pressure from the System
The first advantage Paul cited is this: "In view of the present
distress . . . it is good for a man to remain as he is" (v. 26). It
is natural for a new Christian to encounter some degree of
conflict with the ungodly system. Persecution is difficult
enough for a single person, but the problems and pain are

multiplied for one who is married.

If Paul had been married, his suffering would have been magnified. He would have been concerned about his family, and tormented knowing they were concerned about him. They would have suffered every time he was beaten, stoned, and imprisoned and would have been constantly fearful for his life. Who would have taken care of them in his absence? His practical problems would have increased and the effectiveness of his ministry would have decreased. Married believers who go through some degree of social turmoil cannot escape carrying a much heavier load than those who are single.

Fewer Problems of the Flesh

Single people who choose to marry are certainly free to do so, "yet such will have trouble in this life" (v. 28). We all are subject to fleshly limitations. It is hard enough for a sinner to live with himself, let alone with another sinner. The problems of human nature are multiplied in marriage. When you add children to the mix, who are born sinful, they will have some measure of conflict with each other and their parents.

Even in the best of marriages, each marriage partner has some degree of anger, selfishness, dishonesty, pride, forgetfulness, and thoughtlessness. If God has given you the gift of singleness, it is better to stay that way to avoid the problems our humanness brings into marriage.

Marriage should not be viewed merely as a means of escape. Loneliness and sexual temptation are not eradicated once you've found a life partner. Marriage is the right course of action for one reason only: fulfilling the will of God.

More Detachment from This Passing World

Marriage, as wonderful as it is, will pass away with the world someday, along with weeping, earthly rejoicing, and ownership (vv. 29-32). Godly marriages are "made in heaven," but they will not carry over into heaven. That thought bothers many people because they assume that when they marry, they will always be married. But marriage is not eternal.

Jesus said, "In the resurrection [people] neither marry, nor are given in marriage, but are like angels in heaven" (Matt.

22:30). Although angels do not procreate, they are usually identified by male gender in Scripture, and when they appear, they appear in male form. Because of that and because the resurrected Jesus retained His gender, we can surmise we will retain our gender in eternity. So why will there be no marriage in heaven? Because it won't be necessary. God created marriage because man needed a helper, woman needed a protector, and together both were to produce children. In heaven, man won't need a helper because he will be perfect. Woman won't need a protector because she will be perfect. And no one will be born in heaven because only the redeemed can live there.

Someone might be thinking, *But I'm happily married. I love my wife. She's my best friend and my dearest companion in every area of life.* That's good! You will enjoy that companionship with her in heaven forever – and with every other person in heaven as well. Heaven is one place where there will be no partiality: We will love everyone there equally.

Those who remain single can have a head start now in getting a taste of that heavenly reality. Nevertheless, the focus of all Christians, whether married or single, should be "on the things above, not on the things that are on earth" (Col. 3:2). The Apostle John warned every believer, "Do not love the world, nor the things in the world. If anyone loves the world, the love of the Father is not in him. . . . And the world is passing away, and also its lusts; but the one who does the will of God abides forever" (1 John 2:15, 17). You can love your spouse and at the same time keep your priorities for God in proper perspective.

Freedom from the Preoccupations of Marriage
There are certain cares that encumber your mind when you're married. As Paul put it, "He who is married is concerned about the things of the world, how he may please his wife" (1 Cor. 7:33). You need life insurance so that if you die suddenly, your family will be provided for. As your family grows, you're likely to need a bigger house and car. You'll also need to save money for your children's education. On top of all that, you need to be sensitive to the emotional and

spiritual needs of your family.

A single person, however, "is concerned about the things of the Lord, how he may please the Lord" (v. 32). That doesn't mean, of course, that all single people are more devoted to Jesus Christ, but that the single person has the potential for that kind of devotion. He has but one set of cares: his own, which hopefully are the same as God's. The married person, on the other hand, has a divided set of cares: those of the Lord, and those of his family. It isn't that those divided interests are bad; they're by the design of God. However, inherent in marriage is the inability for singlemindedness.

When I was in Quito, Ecuador, I had the privilege of meeting Rachel Saint, a single woman who has given her life to discipling the Auca Indians. By the grace of God, she and many like her are completely devoted to the Lord without encumbrance. I often think that *those gifted with singleness are possibly the most fulfilled people of all* because they don't need someone else to make them complete.

Not Being Bound to a Lifelong Relationship
Paul concluded his discussion of singleness with this final point: "A wife is bound as long as her husband lives; but if her husband is dead, she is free to be married to whom she wishes, only in the Lord. But in my opinion she is happier if she remains as she is; and I think that I also have the Spirit of God" (vv. 39-40). In other words, since marriage is a lifelong commitment, think seriously before marrying.

Widowed believers are not bound to stay single, but if they remarry, it must be to another believer; "evangelistic" dating is not a legitimate undertaking from God's perspective. Christians are to marry only those in the family of God (9:5; 2 Cor. 6:14; Deut. 7:1-4).

In recommending singleness, Paul is not issuing a command, but is offering counsel. We need to consider it carefully since he speaks as "an apostle of Jesus Christ by the will of God" (1 Cor. 1:1). His convictions and advice on singleness and marriage—and all other matters—are that of the Lord Himself.

The message of 1 Corinthians 7 is that those who possess God's special grace for singleness will be happier if they remain single, and all others will be happier if they marry as God leads. Marriage does not prevent great devotion to Christ, nor does singleness guarantee it, but by definition it is easier for a single person to be singleminded in the things of the Lord. Perhaps God will call or has called you to experience "the grace of life" (1 Peter 3:7). Perhaps He will not spare you "trouble in this life" (1 Cor. 7:28). Whatever your situation, be content to remain as you are—a point Paul makes four separate times in 1 Corinthians 7 (vv. 17, 20, 24, 26)—all the while doing your best to serve God and His people in this life. The bonds of love you cultivate now will spill over to perfection in the next life.

PART THREE

God's Design
for the Church

CHAPTER 6

The Church's
Leading Men

If you were to pick a neighborhood church to visit at random on a Sunday morning, you might find a much different scene than you would have twenty-five years ago. Depending on which denomination you visit, you'd have as much as a 12 percent chance of finding a woman leading the congregation in the worship service, whether reading a Scripture passage or preaching the sermon. And that percentage is likely to increase, not decrease.

Our society gives hearty approval to this trend. Check out this lead from a chapter titled "To Hell with Sexism: Women in Religion" in *Megatrends for Women:*

Women of the late 20th century are revolutionizing the most sexist institution in history—organized religion. Overturning millennia of tradition, they are challenging authorities, reinterpreting the Bible, creating their own services, crowding into seminaries, winning the right to

ordination, purging sexist language in liturgy, reintegrat-
ing female values and assuming positions of leadership
(Patricia Aburdene and John Naisbitt [New York: Fawcett
Columbine, 1992], 119).

The authors then proceed to document each of those activities. A few samples are worth noting.

• "According to a '*USA Today* Snapshot' published March
29, 1993, women account for 12 percent of Episcopal priests,
Presbyterian ministers and Reform Jewish rabbis, as well as
11 percent of Methodist ministers. Women are 9 percent of
Baptist pastors and 2 percent of Conservative Jewish rabbis"
(p. 128).

• "The ranks of fully ordained American women *doubled*
between 1977 and 1986, to 21,000 . . . there are more than
30,000 women ministers today. The figure of 21,000 is well
on its way to doubling again, to 42,000, sometime in the late
1990's" (p. 128, emphasis in original).

• "In 1987 women represented less than 10 percent of the
profession. But in the coming years that percentage will
reach a critical mass of 25 to 30 percent. The reason: a huge
increase in women seminarians" (p. 129).

• "One third of the 56,000 students in seminaries accredit-
ed by the Association of Theological Schools are women,
compared with one eighth 10 years ago and almost none
twenty years ago" (p. 129).

Add to those statistics these disturbing trends: The emerg-
ing feminist theology teaches that God is not male, God does
not exist in a trinitarian form, Jesus was a feminist, and the
true history of women was edited out of the Bible. Female
values are also on the cutting edge: Aburdene and Naisbitt,
the editors of *Megatrends for Women,* assert that once wom-
en's perspectives "attain greater power, [that] will signal rev-
olutionary changes in church policies" (p. 133). And for years
now we have seen a surge in attempts to purge male terminology out of Bible translations.

All this is not limited to liberal churches and denomina-
tions, however. Aburdene and Naisbitt quote in a positive
light Christians for Biblical Equality (the organization we re-

ferred to in chap. 1) for stating that "women as well as men exercise the prophetic, priestly, and royal functions" of the church (p. 128, quoted from "Women Served as Priests," *Grand Rapids Press,* November 9, 1991). Evangelical churches are just as susceptible to the feminist onslaught, and once it gains a foothold, we could very well see similar trends develop within the evangelical community throughout the next twenty years.

At stake today is God's perfect design for His church—a design that reflects the principle of authority and submission operative in both society and the family. While there is no disputing the equality of men and women as believers in Christ, God specifically calls qualified men to lead His church. Women have unique opportunities for service in the church and are in many ways its warmth and depth, but God's basic design for leadership for the church is for men to be in authority. To see how His plan for the roles of men and women in the church fleshes out, we need to turn to the New Testament. A most definitive text is found in Paul's first letter to Timothy. The entire letter focuses on establishing God's standard for order in the life of the church.

PRAYER

In 1 Timothy 2:8 Paul opens with this duty for men: "Therefore I want the men in every place to pray, lifting up holy hands, without wrath and dissension." That text sets the backdrop for the call to pray. "Therefore" refers to the first seven verses of 1 Timothy 2, which discuss the importance of praying for all people—especially non-Christian authorities. The unique responsibility of offering public prayer on behalf of the lost is the special duty for men. The immediately preceding context makes it clear that salvation is the issue:

> First of all, then, I urge that entreaties and prayers, petitions and thanksgivings, be made on behalf of all men, for kings and all who are in authority, in order that we may lead a tranquil and quiet life in all godliness and dignity. This is good and acceptable in the sight of God our Savior, who desires all men to be saved and to come

to the knowledge of the truth. For there is one God, and one mediator also between God and men, the man Christ Jesus, who gave Himself as a ransom for all, the testimony borne at the proper time. And for this I was appointed a preacher and an apostle (I am telling the truth, I am not lying) as a teacher of the Gentiles in faith and truth (vv. 1-7).

The Greek word translated "men" in verse 8 refers to man not in the generic sense, but to men in contrast to women. Men are to be the leaders when the church meets for corporate worship. In the Jewish synagogue, only men were permitted to pray, and that practice was continued in the church. The Greek phrase translated "in every place" refers to an official assembly of the church (1 Cor. 1:2; 2 Cor. 2:14; 1 Thes. 1:8). Paul was saying that no matter where the church officially gathers, select men are to lead in public prayer.

Some claim that contradicts 1 Corinthians 11:5, where Paul permits women to pray and proclaim the Word. That passage, however, must be interpreted in light of 1 Corinthians 14:34, which forbids women to speak in the assembly. And as we found in chapter 2, women *are* permitted to pray and proclaim the Word, but not when the church meets for its official worship service. That in no way marks women as spiritually inferior (cf. Gal. 3:28) — not all men proclaim the Word in the assembly, only those called and gifted to do so.

"Lifting up holy hands, without wrath and dissension" specifies how those men are to pray. It was customary for the Israelites to lift their hands as they prayed (e.g., Ps. 134:2) as a gesture indicating the offering up of prayer and the readiness to receive the answer. The emphasis in the command is not to lift our literal hands, but that our worship must be offered in *holiness*. Thus it stands as a metaphor expressing purity of life. Here we see a specific qualification for the men selected to lead in prayer in public worship: they must live holy lives. And their inner attitude is "without wrath and dissension." Church leaders are not characterized by anger and strife; they are to have loving, peacemaking hearts. Leading the congregation to God is a priestly function. As in the

Old Testament, all priests who led the people to God in public worship were men (Ex. 28:1; 32:26-29; Lev. 8:2; Num. 8:16-26).

LEADERSHIP

Not everyone is cut out for leadership in the church. That's why Paul in 1 Timothy 3:1-7 expands on his instruction for men by describing the categories and qualifications for church leadership. After directing some instruction to the women in the church (which we will examine in the next chapter), Paul says, "It is a trustworthy statement: if any man aspires to the office of overseer, it is a fine work he desires to do" (v. 1).

An essential requirement for a church leader is that he be a man. The indefinite pronoun *tis* ("any man") should be taken here as masculine, in agreement with the masculine form of the adjectives in verses 2-6. Also, a woman could hardly be a "one-woman man" (v. 2), nor did women in that day head households (vv. 5-6). Women have a vitally important role in the church, the home, and in society. That role, however, does not include leadership over God's people. While both men and women can serve in a variety of ways under the general and broad category of deacon (vv. 8-13), Paul makes it clear that the leadership of the church is limited to men.

"Overseer" refers to those men who are called by God to lead His church. In the New Testament the terms "overseer," "pastor," and "elder" all refer to the same office (cf. Acts 20:28; Titus 1:5-9; 1 Peter 5:1-2). Among their responsibilities are ruling, preaching, and teaching (1 Tim. 5:17), praying for the sick (James 5:14), caring for the church, and setting an example for the people to follow (1 Peter 5:1-2), setting church policy (Acts 15:22ff.), and ordaining other leaders (1 Tim. 4:14).

The character and effectiveness of any church is directly related to the quality of its leadership. That's why the Bible stresses the importance of qualified church leadership and delineates specific standards for evaluating those who would serve in that sacred position. Failure to adhere to those standards has caused many of the problems that churches throughout the world currently face.

Significantly, Paul's description of the qualifications for overseers focused on their character rather than their function. That's because a man is qualified by who he *is*, not by what he *does*. If he sins, he is subject to discipline in front of the whole congregation (5:20). The church must carefully guard the integrity of its leadership.

The spiritual qualifications for leadership are nonnegotiable. I am convinced they are part of what determines whether a man is indeed called by God to the ministry. Bible schools and seminaries can help equip a man for ministry, church boards and pulpit committees can extend opportunities for him to serve, but only God can call a man and make him fit for the ministry. And that call is not a matter of analyzing one's talents and then selecting the best career option. It's a Spirit-generated compulsion to be a man of God and serve Him in the church. Those whom God calls will meet the qualifications.

Why are the standards set so high? Because whatever the leaders are, the people become. As Hosea said, "Like people, like priest" (4:9). Jesus said, "Everyone, after he has been fully trained, will be like his teacher" (Luke 6:40). Biblical history demonstrates that people will seldom rise above the spiritual level of their leadership.

Some of you might be thinking that these qualifications don't apply to you because you don't sense God's call. Yet the only significant difference between an elder's qualifications and those of a deacon is that an elder must be skilled as a teacher (cf. 1 Tim. 3:1-7 and 8-13). In addition, Paul applies most of these character qualities to all believers in his other letters. So in that sense, whether you are male or female, these qualities ought to be the goals in your Christian life. But if you are a man seeking a position of leadership, you must meet the required qualifications.

Paul begins by asserting that the man who desires the office desires a good work (v. 1), but no one should ever be placed into church leadership on desire alone. It is the church's responsibility to affirm a man's qualifications for ministry by measuring him against God's standard for leadership as delineated in verses 2-7.

Above Reproach

A fundamental, universal requirement for an overseer is that he "must be above reproach" (v. 2). It is an absolute necessity. The Greek text indicates that being above reproach is the man's present state — he has sustained a reputation for being irreproachable. There's nothing to accuse him of. It doesn't refer to sins he committed before he matured as a Christian — unless those sins remain a blight on his life.

A church leader's life must not be marred by sin or vice — be it an attitude, habit, or incident. That's not to say he must be perfect, but there must not be any obvious defect in his character. He must be a model of godliness so he can legitimately call his congregation to follow his example (Phil. 3:17). That is a high standard, but it isn't a double standard. Since you are responsible to follow the example of your godly leaders (Heb. 13:7, 17), God requires you to be above reproach as well. The difference is that certain sins can disqualify church leaders for life, whereas that's not necessarily true for less prominent roles in the church. Nevertheless, God requires blamelessness of all believers (cf. Eph. 1:4; Phil. 1:10; Col. 1:22; 2 Peter 3:14; Jude 24).

A church leader disqualifies himself when his unrighteousness communicates to others that one can live in sin and still be a spiritual leader. Malicious people are always looking for ways to discredit the reputation of Christ and His church. A sinful leader plays right into their hands, giving them an unparalleled opportunity to justify their lack of belief.

It's not coincidental that many pastors fall into sin and disqualify themselves from ministry. Satan works hard at undermining the integrity of spiritual leaders because in so doing, he destroys their ministries and brings reproach upon Christ. Therefore spiritual leaders must guard their thoughts and actions carefully, and congregations must pray earnestly for the strength of their leadership. An unholy pastor is like a stained glass window: a religious symbol that obscures the light. That's why the initial qualification for spiritual leadership is blamelessness. As Paul delineates the other qualifications for overseers, he simply expands on the particulars of what it means to be above reproach.

Moral Qualifications

Paul initially lists several moral qualifications for an elder: He is to be "the husband of one wife, temperate, prudent, respectable, hospitable, able to teach, not addicted to wine or pugnacious, but gentle, uncontentious, free from the love of money" (1 Tim. 3:2-3).

Sexual Purity

A leader must first be "the husband of one wife." The Greek text literally reads "a one-woman man." That phrase doesn't refer to marital status at all but to his moral character regarding his sexual behavior. If he is married, he is to be devoted solely to his wife (cf. 1 Tim. 5:9).

It is possible, however, to be married to one woman yet not be a one-woman man. Jesus said, "Everyone who looks on a woman to lust for her has committed adultery with her already in his heart" (Matt. 5:28). A married — or unmarried — man who lusts after women is unfit for ministry. An elder must love, desire, and think only of the wife God has given him.

That qualification was especially important in Ephesus, where sexual evil was rampant. Many, if not most, of the congregation had at one time or another fallen prey to sexual evil. If that was a man's experience before he came to Christ, it wasn't a problem (cf. 2 Cor. 5:17). If it happened after his conversion, but before he assumed a leadership role, it was a problem. If it happened after he assumed a leadership role, it was a definite disqualification (1 Cor. 9:24-27). Those same standards apply to men in positions of spiritual leadership today.

Sexual purity is a major issue in ministry, and that's why Paul placed it at the top of his list. It is in this arena, above all others, where leaders are most prone to fall. The inability to be a one-woman man may have put more men out of the ministry than any other issue.

Not Given to Excess

A leader in God's church must also be "temperate." The Greek word translated "temperate" *(nēphalios)* means "with-

The Church's Leading Men   117

out wine" or "not mixed with wine." It refers to sobriety, the opposite of intoxication. Because Palestine was so hot and dry, wine was a common drink. Although usually diluted with large amounts of water, the lack of refrigeration and wine's fermentative properties meant intoxication could be a problem.

Even though wine can cheer a person's heart (Jud. 9:13), and was beneficial for medicinal purposes such as stomach ailments (1 Tim. 5:23) and relieving pain for those near death (Prov. 31:6), its abuse was common. As Proverbs 20:1 says, "Wine is a mocker, strong drink a brawler, and whoever is intoxicated by it is not wise."

Because of their position, example, and influence, certain Jewish leaders abstained from wine. Priests were not to enter God's house while under its influence (Lev. 10:9). Kings were advised not to consume wine because it might hinder their judgment (Prov. 31:4-5). The Nazirite vow, the highest vow of spiritual commitment in the Old Testament, forbade its participants from drinking wine (Num. 6:3). In the same way, spiritual leaders today must avoid intoxication so that they might exercise responsible judgment and set an example of Spirit-controlled behavior.

It's likely Paul's primary usage of *nēphalios* went beyond the literal sense of avoiding intoxication to the figurative sense of being alert and watchful. An elder must deny any excess in life that diminishes clear thinking and sound judgment. Commentator William Hendriksen said, "His pleasures are not primarily those of the senses . . . but those of the soul" *(Exposition of the Pastoral Epistles* [Grand Rapids: Baker, 1981], 122).

Drinking is only one area in which excess can occur. Overeating has been called the preacher's sin, and often that's a just criticism. Spiritual leaders must be moderate and balanced in every area of life.

Self-disciplined

It follows that a "temperate" leader will be "prudent," or self-disciplined. The temperate man avoids excess so he can think clearly, which leads to an orderly, disciplined life. He knows how to order his priorities.

A "prudent" man is serious about spiritual things. That doesn't mean he is cold and humorless, but he tempers his humor by the realities of the world. A world that is lost, disobedient to God, and bound for hell leaves little room for frivolity in his ministry.

Such a man has a sure and steady mind. He is not rash in judgment, but thoughtful, earnest, and cautious. He follows Paul's counsel in Philippians 4:8: "Whatever is true, whatever is honorable, whatever is right, whatever is pure, whatever is lovely, whatever is of good repute, if there is any excellence and if anything worthy of praise, let your mind dwell on these things." His mind is controlled by God's truth, not the whims of the flesh. Jesus Christ reigns supreme over every area of his life.

Well-organized

It follows that a man who is prudent will have a "respectable" or orderly life. That means he handles every area of his life in a systematic, orderly manner. His well-disciplined mind leads to a well-disciplined life.

The Greek word translated "respectable" is *kosmios* and derives from the root *kosmos*. The opposite of *kosmos* is "chaos." A spiritual leader must not live in a chaotic but in an orderly fashion since his work involves administration, oversight, scheduling, and establishing priorities.

The ministry is no place for a man whose life is a continual confusion of unaccomplished plans and unorganized activities. Over the years I have seen many men who had difficulty ministering effectively because they were unable to concentrate on a task or systematically set and accomplish goals. Such disorder is a disqualification.

Hospitable

The Greek word translated "hospitable" is composed of the words *xenos* ("stranger") and *phileō* ("to love" or "show affection"). It means "to love strangers." Thus biblical hospitality is showing kindness to strangers, not friends. In Luke 14:12-14 our Lord said,

When you give a luncheon or a dinner, do not invite
your friends or your brothers or your relatives or rich
neighbors, lest they also invite you in return, and repay-
ment come to you. But when you give a reception, invite the poor, the crippled, the lame, the blind, and you
will be blessed, since they do not have the means to
repay you; for you will be repaid at the resurrection of
the righteous.

I realize that showing love toward strangers requires vulnerability, and can even be dangerous because some may
take advantage of your kindness. While God doesn't ask us to
discard wisdom and discernment in dealing with strangers (cf.
Matt. 10:16), He does require us to love them by being hospitable (Rom. 12:13; Heb. 13:2; 1 Peter 4:9).

When I consider my responsibility to love strangers, I am
reminded that God received into His family we who were
"excluded from the commonwealth of Israel, and strangers to
the covenants of promise, having no hope and without God in
the world" (Eph. 2:12). Since those of us who are Gentiles
have been welcomed by God, how can we fail to welcome
strangers into our homes? After all, everything we have belongs to God. We are simply His stewards.

A Skilled Teacher

The Greek word translated "able to teach" *(didaktikos)* is
used only two times in the New Testament (1 Tim. 3:2 and in
2 Tim. 2:24). An elder must be a skilled teacher. That's the
one qualification that sets him apart from deacons and the
rest of the congregation.

Some may wonder why Paul includes this qualification in
the midst of a list of moral qualities. He does so because
effective teaching is predicated on the moral character of the
teacher. What a man *is* cannot be divorced from what he says.
"He that means as he speaks," writes Richard Baxter, "will
surely do as he speaks" *(The Reformed Pastor* [Edinburgh:
Banner of Truth, 1979], 63).

Paul repeatedly reminded Timothy of the priority of teaching (1 Tim. 5:17; 2 Tim. 2:2, 15). While all believers are

responsible to teach others the truths they have learned in God's Word, not all have the gift of teaching (1 Cor. 12:29). Those who aspire to church leadership, however, must be so gifted.

What criteria identify a man as a skilled teacher? There are several:

● He must be credible and live what he teaches (1 Tim. 4:12).

● He must have the gift of teaching (1 Tim. 4:14; 2 Tim. 1:6).

● He must have a deep understanding of doctrine (1 Tim. 4:6).

● He must have an attitude of humility (2 Tim. 2:24-25).

● His life must be marked by holiness (1 Tim. 4:7; 6:11).

● He must be a diligent student of Scripture (2 Tim. 2:15).

● He must avoid error (1 Tim. 4:7; 6:20; 2 Tim. 2:16).

● He must have strong courage and consistent convictions (cf. 1 Tim. 1:18-19; 4:11, 13).

Not a Drinker

The Greek word translated "addicted to wine" *(paroinos)* means "one who drinks." It doesn't refer to a drunkard— that's an obvious disqualification. The issue here is the man's reputation: Is he known as a drinker?

We found that the Greek word translated "temperate" (1 Tim. 3:3) refers in its literal sense to one who is not intoxicated. *Paroinos,* on the other hand, refers to one's associations: Such a person doesn't frequent bars, taverns, and inns. He is not at home in the noisy scenes associated with drinking. A man who is a drinker has no place in the ministry because he sets a poor example for others by choosing to fellowship with evil men instead of God's people.

Not a Fighter

A leader of God's people cannot settle disputes with his fists or in other violent ways. The Greek word translated "pugnacious" means "a giver of blows" or "a striker." An elder isn't quick tempered and doesn't resort to physical violence. This qualification is closely related to "not addicted to wine" because such violence is usually connected with people who drink excessively.

A spiritual leader must be able to handle things with a cool mind and a gentle spirit. As Paul said, "The Lord's bondservant must not be quarrelsome" (2 Tim. 2:24).

Easily Pardons Human Failure

Instead of being pugnacious, a leader must be "gentle." The Greek word translated "gentle" describes the person who is considerate, genial, forbearing, gracious, and easily pardons human failure.

In a practical sense, a gentle leader has the ability to remember good and forget evil. He doesn't keep a record of wrongs people have committed against him (cf. 1 Cor. 13:5). I know people who have left the ministry because they couldn't get over someone's criticizing or upsetting them. They carry a list of grievances that eventually robs them of the joy of serving others.

Discipline yourself not to talk or even think about wrongs done against you because it serves no productive purpose. It simply rehearses the hurts and clouds your mind with anger.

Not Quarrelsome

The Greek word translated "uncontentious" means "peaceful" or "reluctant to fight." It refers not so much to physical violence as to a quarrelsome person. To have a contentious person in leadership will result in disunity and disharmony.

Free from the Love of Money

Love of money can corrupt a man's ministry because it tempts him to view people as a means through whom he can acquire more riches. Here's a simple principle I've used to keep from loving money: Don't place a price on your ministry.

If someone gives you a financial gift you didn't seek, you can accept it from the Lord and be thankful for it. But if you pursue money, you'll never know if it came from Him or from your own efforts, and that will rob you of the joy of seeing God provide for your needs.

Family Leadership

First Timothy 3:4-5 adds that an overseer must be "one who manages his own household well, keeping his children under control with all dignity (but if a man does not know how to manage his own household, how will he take care of the church of God?)." An elder's home life is an essential consideration. Before he can lead in the church he must demonstrate his spiritual leadership within the context of his family.

The Greek word translated "manages" means "to preside" or "to have authority over." The same Greek word is translated "rule" in 5:17 in reference to elders leading in the church. An elder's ability to rule the church is affirmed in his home. Therefore he must be a strong spiritual leader there before he is qualified to lead in the church.

Many men rule their home but don't rule it very well—they don't get the desired results. By implication a man's home includes his resources. A man may be spiritually and morally qualified to be an elder, be skilled in teaching, and have a believing wife and children who follow his leadership in the home, but if he doesn't rule his household well in the financial realm, he is disqualified from spiritual leadership. Stewardship of possessions is a critical test of a man's leadership. His home is the proving ground where his leadership capabilities can be clearly demonstrated.

Further, a leader in the church must keep "his children under control with all dignity." That qualification is not meant to exclude men without children, but merely assumes they will be present. The Greek word translated "under control" is a military term that refers to lining up in rank under those in authority. "Dignity" includes courtesy, humility, and competence. It could be translated "respect," or "stateliness." An elder's children are to be respectful and well-disciplined, bringing honor to their parents.

In Titus 1:6 Paul adds that an elder must have "children who believe, not accused of dissipation or rebellion." The Greek word translated "believe" refers in that context to believing the Gospel. An elder's children must believe the message he's preaching and teaching. If they are unbelievers, they rob his ministry of credibility.

There's no better place to see a man's commitment to meeting the needs of others than in his own home. Does he care about his family? Is he committed to each member? Does he work hard to meet their needs? Have they followed his faith?

Spiritual Maturity

Although Paul didn't specifically mention humility in this passage, it is the obvious point of contrast in his caution against spiritual pride. An elder must not be "a new convert, lest he become conceited and fall into the condemnation incurred by the devil" (1 Tim. 3:6).

The Greek word translated "new convert" means "newly planted." An elder should not be a new convert or newly baptized. Instead, he must be mature in the faith. Since maturity is relative, the standard of maturity will vary from congregation to congregation. But the point is that an elder must be more spiritually mature than the people he leads.

The Greek word translated "lifted up" means "to wrap in smoke" or "to puff up." In its figurative sense it refers to being clouded with pride. New Christians must guard against pride revealed in a false sense of spirituality.

Restricting a new convert from spiritual leadership is not an indictment on his teaching ability, leadership qualities, or his knowledge of God's Word. But elevating him to spiritual leadership alongside mature godly men will cause him to battle with pride.

You might expect Paul to say that prideful leaders will become ineffective or fall into sin, but instead he says they will fall "into the condemnation of the devil." That's a reference to the judgment God pronounced on Lucifer, the devil. A prideful leader will incur that same type of condemnation, which is a demotion from a high position. God will do the same to any man whose thinking is clouded by pride and whose perception of his own spirituality is distorted because of a premature rise to spiritual leadership.

The antidote to pride is humility, which is the mark of a spiritually mature leader (Matt. 23:11-12). The church must not lift up those whom the Lord may later have to cut down.

Public Reputation

The godly character of an elder must not be manifested only in the church and his home; he must also "have a good reputation with those outside the church, so that he may not fall into reproach and the snare of the devil" (1 Tim. 3:7). "Reputation" translates *marturia,* from which derives the English word "martyr," and refers to a certifying testimony. A man chosen to lead the church must have a reputation in the community for righteousness, love, kindness, generosity, and goodness. All people won't agree with his theology, and he will no doubt face antagonism when he takes a stand for God's truth. Nevertheless, those outside the church must recognize him as a man of impeccable reputation. How can any man have an impact on his community if that community does not respect him? Such an individual can do nothing but bring "reproach" or disgrace on the cause of Christ.

I can't count how many men have disgraced the Lord and His church because of their sins. That's why an elder must be blameless in his reputation. Incidently, this qualification isn't limited to sins committed as an elder; it also takes into account any sins in the past that result in a bad reputation. A man's ongoing reputation in the community must be considered before he is placed into spiritual leadership.

Every Christian has to deal with some level of visibility. And people need to see a blameless life. They may not agree with your beliefs, but they must see your godly character.

Elders need a good reputation with those outside the church so they don't fall into "the snare of the devil." Satan tries hard to entrap spiritual leaders to destroy their credibility and integrity. Like all Christians, elders have areas of weakness and vulnerability, and they will sometimes fall into one of his traps. Only a perfect man doesn't stumble (James 3:2). Elders must be particularly discerning and cautious to avoid the snares of the enemy so they can be effective in leading others away from his traps.

A CALL TO WORK

Many contemporary church leaders fancy themselves businessmen, executives, entertainers, psychologists, philosophers, presidents, or lawyers. Yet those roles contrast sharply with the symbolism Scripture employs to depict pastors and spiritual leaders in the church. In 2 Timothy 2, for example, Paul uses seven different metaphors to describe a spiritual leader. He pictures the minister as a teacher (v. 2), a soldier (v. 3), an athlete (v. 5), a farmer (v. 6), a workman (v. 15), a vessel (vv. 20-21), and a slave (v. 24). Each of those images evokes ideas of sacrifice, labor, service, and hardship. They speak eloquently about the complex and varied responsibilities of spiritual leadership. Not one of them makes out leadership to be glamorous.

That's because it's not supposed to be glamorous. Leadership in the church is not a mantle of status to be conferred on the church's aristocracy. It isn't earned by seniority, purchased with money, or inherited through family ties. It doesn't necessarily fall to those who are successful in business or finance. It isn't doled out on the basis of intelligence, education, or talent. Its requirements are faultless character, spiritual maturity, skill in teaching, and a willingness to serve humbly.

God has ordained that leadership is to be a role of humble, loving service. Church leadership is ministry, not management. God calls leaders not to be governing monarchs but humble slaves, not slick celebrities but laboring servants, not charismatic personalities but faithful shepherds. The man who leads God's people must above all exemplify sacrifice, devotion, submission, and lowliness.

With the trends in the church headed where they are, nothing is more sorely needed today than a return to biblical leadership principles. Solid men willing to take on the true realities of leadership are appallingly rare, yet they are needed more than ever to stop the inexorable march of feminine values.

Let American President Theodore Roosevelt's words be your inspiration:

It is not the critic who counts; not the man who points out how the strong man stumbled or where the doer of the deed could have done better. The credit belongs to the man who is actually in the arena, whose face is marred by dust and sweat and blood, who strives valiantly; who errs, and comes short again and again, because there is no effort without error and shortcoming; who does actually try to do the deed; who knows the great enthusiasm, the great devotion and spends himself in a worthy cause; who, at the worst, if he fails, at least he fails while daring greatly.

Far better is it to dare mighty things, to win glorious triumphs even though checked by failure, than to rank with those poor spirits who neither enjoy nor suffer much because they live in a gray twilight that knows little victory nor defeat (cf. Hamilton Club speech, Chicago, 10 Apr. 1899).

CHAPTER 7

God's High Call
for Women

No other passage of Scripture has been subject to more scrutiny in the ongoing feminist debate over the role of women in the church than 1 Timothy 2:9-15. Not just chapters, but entire books have been devoted to refuting the historical and traditional interpretations of this important passage (e.g. R.C. Kroeger and C.C. Kroeger, *I Suffer Not a Woman* [Grand Rapids: Baker, 1992]).

To capsulize the variety of interpretations from evangelical and charismatic feminists, J. David Pawson offers this revealing paraphrase:

Verse 11: You must teach women so that they can become teachers themselves; as with men under instructions, the women also must not interrupt with aggressive opinions of their own.

Verse 12: Personally, I don't make a practice of letting women teach because hitherto they have not had the educational opportunity to study the Scriptures; asserting their somewhat ignorant ideas in an authoritarian manner could be seen as putting down their husbands.

Verse 13: Nevertheless, when Adam was created, he was immediately given a colleague to complete and complement him as a coequal, sharing fully his dual role of ruling the world and teaching others the word of God.

Verse 14: Satan was able to deceive Eve only because she was not present when God spoke to Adam and she had only a second-hand report of what was said; Adam, on the other hand, knew better and his sin, unlike hers, was inexcusable.

Verse 15: This is why God spoke so tenderly to Eve, promising to vindicate her innocence and save her from undeserved dishonor and shame by choosing a woman to bear that special Child who would defeat Satan and thus save all women of faith, love, holiness, and good sense (*Leadership Is Male* [Nashville: Thomas Nelson, 1990], 82–83).

Others, such as Gretchen Gaebelein Hull, don't want to even deal with passages like this one and 1 Corinthians 11:2-16 and 14:33-35 because they are too "hard" to interpret (*Equal to Serve: Women and Men in the Church and Home* [Old Tappan, N.J.: Fleming H. Revell, 1987], 183–89). Hull even adds Ephesians 5:22-24, Colossians 3:18, and 1 Peter 3:1-6 to the list. In her attempt to prove that the Bible does not teach male headship, she is forced to dispose of those passages that indeed teach male headship. Hull concludes, "Those of us who respect God's Word cannot force meaning where meaning is unclear. Therefore we may legitimately put these Scripture portions aside for the very reason that they *remain* 'hard passages' — hard exegetically, hard hermeneutically, and hard theologically" (p. 189).

If all theologians were to follow that principle of interpretation, Satan wouldn't need to attack the truthfulness of Scripture; he would only have to cause enough confusion over the "hard passages" for scholars to ignore them. John W. Robbins explains the tragedy of such an approach:

The demand for the ordination of women, as rebellious as it is in itself, is a symptom of a much more serious malady. The ordination of women might disfigure the church, but the disease of which it is a symptom will kill her unless it is quickly diagnosed and treated. That disease . . . is the rejection of Biblical inerrancy.

[One seminary professor] entertains the possibility that Paul contradicts himself. [Another] asserts that the Bible contains "antinomies," a polite word for contradictions. [Yet another] picks and chooses which of the Biblical requirements for elders he is going to tolerate. . . . If the rest of Scripture, the passages concerning the Trinity, Christ's deity, or justification through faith alone, for example, were subjected to the same exegetical mayhem as wreaked on I Corinthians and I Timothy, there would be no truth at all in our theology (*Scripture Twisting in the Seminaries, Part One: Feminism,* "The Most Serious Error" [Jefferson, Md.: The Trinity Foundation, 1985], 51, 53).

As we've noted in previous chapters, some evangelical feminists assert that Paul was simply dealing with a cultural issue and never intended his instruction to go beyond that. Among those in this camp are the Kroegers. Peter Jones comments on their book *I Suffer Not a Woman:*

The great insights of this study concerning Paul's biblical answer to Gnostic distortions is vitiated by the authors' rejection of this answer as applying only to an extreme, first-century situation. The authors fail to see that this same Gnostic heresy is back with a vengeance via the New Age teaching seeping into the contemporary church and society, and that Paul's teaching has perhaps never been more relevant than now (*The Gnostic Empire Strikes Back* [Phillipsburg, N.J.: P. & R., 1992], 41).

Scripture is timeless, thus it is contemporary. Just as God never changes, neither does His Word. It is as active and

living today as it was 2,000 years ago (Heb. 4:12). In spite of
what feminists claim, I believe no passage is more affirming
to and more necessary for women to understand than
1 Timothy 2:9-15. As we move through Paul's words to
Timothy regarding the women in the Ephesian assembly,
you'll find that his commands and restrictions are a means of
great blessing, not a declaration of second-class status.

The church at Ephesus had many problems, one of which
was the role of women. That is not surprising in a church
plagued with false doctrine and false leaders. Some women
were leading impure lives (cf. 5:6, 11-15; 2 Tim. 3:6), and that
indecency carried over into the worship service. Under the
pretense of coming to worship God, some women were
flaunting their wealth and beauty, allowing their sexual allure
to divert the focus from the worship service. Other women,
desirous of being the official teachers, were usurping the role
of men in the church. Their actions revealed their evil intent.
Since worship is central to the life of the church, it was high
on Paul's list of things for Timothy to deal with at Ephesus.

After his discussion of evangelistic prayer in 1 Timothy
2:1-8, Paul turns to the subject of corporate worship. In this
context he provides correction for the two areas of abuses,
and thus establishes timeless guidelines for the behavior of
women when the church meets to worship.

A CORRECTIVE REGARDING DRESS

Paul first instructs Timothy to have the women "adorn themselves with proper clothing, modestly and discreetly, not with
braided hair and gold or pearls or costly garments; but rather
by means of good works, as befits women making a claim to
godliness" (vv. 9-10). That principle is as applicable today as
when it was first established.

Several ancient writers have described how women
dressed in the Roman culture of Paul's day, which no doubt
influenced the church at Ephesus. The writings of Juvenal, a
first-century master of satire, picture everyday life in the
Roman Empire. His sixth satire describes women preoccupied with their appearance: "There is nothing that [such] a
woman will not permit herself to do, nothing that she deems

shameful, and when she encircles her neck with green emeralds and fastens huge pearls to her elongated ears, so important is the business of beautification; so numerous are the tiers and stories piled one another on her head! In the meantime she pays no attention to her husband!"

Pliny the Elder reported that Lollia Paulina, one-time wife of the Roman Emperor Caligula, had a dress worth more than one million dollars by today's standards. It was covered with emeralds and pearls, and she carried with her the receipts proving its value *(Natural History* 9:58).

Wealthy people in ancient times could dress in a style that was impossible for a poor person to match — in contrast to today, where good clothing is affordable for most people in Western societies. A costly dress worn by a wealthy woman of Paul's day could cost up to 7,000 denarii (one denarius was a day's wage for the average laborer). When a woman entered a worship service wearing such a dress, she caused a sensation that would disrupt the entire service.

Rich women also displayed their wealth through elaborate hairdos with expensive jewelry woven into them. That's what Paul meant by "braided hair and gold or pearls" (1 Tim. 2:9). The Bible does not forbid women from wearing simple braids or gold, pearls, and high-quality clothing. Both the bride of Solomon (Song 1:10) and the virtuous woman described in Proverbs 31:22 wore beautiful clothes and jewelry. However, the Bible does forbid wearing those things for wrong motives.

Presenting a Godly Appearance

Wearing expensive clothes and jewelry is inappropriate for women in the church. To come to church so attired is at best a distraction and at worst an attempt to seduce the men. It violates the purpose of the worship service, which is to focus on God. A Christian woman ought to attract attention by her godly character, not her physical beauty.

Timothy was to instruct the women to "adorn themselves with proper clothing." "Adorn" is from *kosmeō,* from which we derive our English word "cosmetic." It means "to arrange," "to put in order," or "to make ready." A woman must prepare herself properly for the worship service. Part of that preparation involves the wearing of "proper clothing." "Proper" translates *kosmiō*, the adjectival form of *kosmeō*, and could be translated "well-ordered." The Greek word translated "clothing" encompasses not only clothing but also demeanor and action. Women are to come to the worship service fully prepared, not in disarray with an unbecoming demeanor or wardrobe. While Paul emphasizes clothing in this passage, the underlying attitude is the real issue. Proper adornment on the outside reflects a proper heart attitude.

How can you discern the sometimes fine line between proper dress and dressing to be the center of attention? The answer lies in the intent of the heart. You should examine your motives and goals for the way you dress. Is your intent to reflect the grace and beauty of womanhood? Is it to show your love and devotion to your husband? Is it to reveal a humble heart devoted to worshiping God? Or is it to call attention to yourself—to flaunt your wealth and beauty? Or worse, to attempt to allure men sexually? The tragic number of pastors who have fallen into immorality indicates that not all women in today's church have entirely pure motives. If you are focused on worshiping God, you won't have to worry about how you dress because your commitment will dictate your wardrobe.

Godly Attitudes

Two attitudes ought to characterize your approach to worship: "modestly and discreetly" (v. 9). The Greek word translated "modestly" in verse 9 refers to modesty mixed with humility. At its core it connotes a sense of shame—not shame in being a woman, but shame for in any way inciting lust or distracting others from a proper worship of God. A godly woman will do all she can to avoid being a source of temptation. The word also has the connotation of rejecting anything dishonorable to God. Some would even suggest it means "grief over a sense of sin." A godly woman hates sin so much that she will avoid anything that can produce sin in others.

"Discreetly" refers to self-control, especially over sexual passions. Women are to have control over their passions, especially in regard to the worship service.

A practical booklet expands our understanding of these two terms by asking us to consider the following dictionary definitions:

- Modest: Having a regard for decencies of behavior or dress; quiet and humble in appearance, style, etc.; not displaying one's body; not boastful or vain; unassuming; virtuous; shy or reserved; chaste.
- Proper: Specially adapted or suitable; appropriate; conforming to an accepted standard; correct; fitting; right; decent.
- Discreet: Lacking ostentation or pretension; showing good judgment; prudent; cautious; careful about what one says or does.

The booklet goes on to state:

Our bodies are precious because they are a gift from God. They are attractive because God made us in His image for His pleasure (and if we are married, to please our mates as well). But God never intended us to flaunt ourselves or exhibit our bodies in an immodest way ... (Rom. 12:1). ...

Many Christians are ... either oblivious or uncaring about the effect they have on others. They may even appear to have a real excitement and love for the Lord— however, their body is sending out a totally different message (Melody Green, "Uncovering the Truth about Modesty" [Lindale, Texas: Last Days Ministries, 1982]).

A Godly Testimony

Paul was greatly concerned that women's testimonies be consistent—that they display "good works, as befits women making a claim to godliness" (1 Tim. 2:10). "Making a claim" is from *epangellō,* which means "to make a public announcement." "Godliness" conveys the basic meaning of reverence to God. Any woman who publicly announces her commitment to Christ should support that declaration with her attitude, appearance, and conduct. She is to be adorned "by means of good works," not by the mere externals discussed in verse 9. "Good" refers to "works" that are genuinely good, not merely good in appearance.

A Christian worships, honors, and fears God. Therefore any woman who claims to be a Christian ought to conduct herself in a godly way. That points out a major problem with the contemporary women's liberation movement in the church. A woman cannot claim to fear God and yet disregard what His Word says about her role. She cannot violate His order for the church in the name of serving Him. Those professing reverence for God will reveal that by their attitude in coming to worship Him.

A CORRECTIVE REGARDING AUTHORITY

Paul next directs his attention to those women in the Ephesian assembly who wanted to take over the teaching roles. In 1 Timothy 2:11-14 he writes, "Let a woman quietly receive instruction with entire submissiveness. But I do not allow a woman to teach or exercise authority over a man, but to remain quiet. For it was Adam who was first created, and then Eve. And it was not Adam who was deceived, but the woman being quite deceived, fell into transgression."

Women Are Learners

Paul begins his corrective by defining women as learners during the worship service. They are not to be teachers in that context, but neither are they to be shut out of the learning process. The verb in verse 11 is an imperative form of *manthanō*, from which the Greek word translated "disciple" derives. Paul commands that the women be taught, or discipled. Since this section of 1 Timothy is discussing how the church is to conduct itself (cf. 3:15), the learning Paul refers to was to take place when the church met (cf. Acts 2:42). Despite the claims of some to the contrary, teaching and worship are not mutually exclusive. Rather, knowledge of God and His Word helps stimulate worship.

While it may seem obvious to us that women should be taught God's Word, that was not true for those (like some at

Ephesus, cf. 1 Tim. 1:7) who came from a Jewish background. First-century Judaism did not esteem women. Although they were not barred from attending synagogue, neither were they encouraged to learn. Even most ancient religions (and some religions existing today) perceive women as unworthy of participating in religious life. Unfortunately that historical treatment of women continues to incite modern feminism.

The traditional treatment of women in Ephesus partially explains why some in the church who overreacted to their suppression by seeking a dominant position. Paul rebukes them for that. Before he does, however, he affirms their right to learn.

A Biblical Survey

The prevalent Jewish tradition about women did not come from the Old Testament, which makes it clear women are spiritually equal to men in that:

• They Had the Same Responsibilities as Men: To obey God's Law (in Ex. 20 the Ten Commandments are given to both men and women), to teach God's Law (Deut. 6:6-7 and Prov. 6:20 indicates both are responsible to teach the Law to their children, which means both must first know it), and to participate in religious festivals (e.g., Ex. 12 and the Passover).

• They Had the Same Protection as Men: Penalties given for crimes against women are the same as those for crimes against men (e.g., Ex. 21:28-32). God equally values the life of a man and the life of a woman.

• They Took the Same Vows as Men: The highest level of spiritual commitment available to an Old Testament believer was the Nazirite vow, which was an act of separation from the world and devotion to God. Women as well as men could take that vow (Num. 6:2).

• They Had the Same Access to God as Men: God dealt directly with women in the Old Testament; He didn't go through a man when He wanted to communicate with a woman. For example, the Angel of the Lord (a preincarnate manifestation of Christ) appeared to Hagar (Gen. 16:8-13) and Samson's mother (Jud. 13:2-5).

Although women shared spiritual equality with men in the Old Testament, they did not have the same role as men:

• They Did Not Serve as Leaders: There were no queens in either Israel or Judah (Athaliah was a usurper). While it is true that Deborah served as a judge (Jud. 4:4–5:31), her case was unique. Dr. Robert L. Saucy comments,

> There may be instances when the regular pattern of God's order may have to be set aside due to unusual circumstances. When, for example, the husband and father is absent, the woman of the house assumes the headship of the family. So it would appear, there may be unusual circumstances when male leadership is unavailable for one reason or another. At such times God may use women to accomplish his purposes even as he used Deborah ("The Negative Case Against the Ordination of Women," in Kenneth S. Kantzer and Stanley N. Gundry, eds. *Perspectives on Evangelical Theology* [Grand Rapids: Baker, 1979], 285).

Deborah acted primarily in the role of an arbiter, not as an ongoing leader, which explains why she called on Barak when needing military leadership against the Canaanites (Jud. 4–5). There is no mention of women priests in the Old Testament. No woman wrote any portion of the Old Testament.

• They Had No Ongoing Prophetic Ministry: No woman in the Old Testament had a prolonged prophetic ministry such as that of Elisha or Elijah. While Miriam (Ex. 15:20), Deborah (Jud. 4:4), Huldah (2 Kings 22:14), and Isaiah's wife (Isa. 8:3) are called prophetesses, none had an ongoing ministry. Miriam, Deborah, and Huldah gave only one recorded prophecy, and Isaiah's wife none. She is called a prophetess because she gave birth to a child whose name had prophetic meaning. A fifth woman mentioned as a prophetess, Noadiah, was a false prophetess (Neh. 6:14). God did speak through women on a few limited occasions, but no woman had an ongoing role of preaching and teaching.

The New Testament, like the Old, teaches the spiritual equality and differing roles of the sexes. As we studied in chapter 2, Galatians 3:28 teaches the absolute spiritual equality of men and women in Christ. The New Testament does not treat women as spiritual inferiors:

• They Had the Same Responsibilities as Men: All the commands, promises, and blessings of the New Testament are given equally to men and women. We have the same spiritual resources and the same spiritual responsibilities.

• They Had the Same Access to Jesus as Men: The first person Jesus revealed His messiahship to in the Gospel record was a woman (John 4). Jesus healed women (Matt. 8:14-15), showing them just as much compassion as He did men. He taught them (Luke 10:38-42), and allowed them to minister to Him personally (8:3). The first person to see the resurrected Christ was a woman (Mark 16:9; John 20:11-18).

The role distinction between men and women is preserved, however, for there is no New Testament record of a woman apostle, pastor, evangelist, or elder. Nowhere in the New Testament does a woman preach any sermon. While the daughters of Philip are said to have prophesied (Acts 21:9), their role is not defined. There is no reason to assume they had an ongoing prophetic ministry, or that they prophesied during the church service. They, like Mary the mother of Jesus (Luke 1:46ff.), or Anna (2:36-38), may have delivered prophecies elsewhere.

Learning Qualified

As we noted in chapter 2, 1 Corinthians 11:5 indicates women are permitted to speak the Word at many times and places, but Paul's instruction in 1 Timothy restricts them from doing so in the official assembly of the church. In 1 Timothy 2:11 he qualifies the way in which women are to be learners: they are to "quietly receive instruction with entire submissiveness." "Submissiveness" translates *hupotagē,* the noun form of *hupotassō,* which we discovered in chapter 2 means "to line up under." In the context of the worship service, then, women are to be quiet and be subject to the church leadership.

Some have tried to evade the plain meaning of the text by arguing that "silently" refers to a woman's meek and quiet spirit. Women, they contend, can preach or teach as long as they do it with the proper attitude. Others go to the opposite extreme and use this text to prohibit women from ever talking in church under any circumstance — even to the person she is sitting next to! Neither of those options is valid, however. The context makes the meaning of "silently" quite clear.

In verse 12, Paul defines what he means: "I do not allow a woman to teach or exercise authority over a man." Women are to keep quiet in the sense of not teaching, and they are to demonstrate subjection by not usurping authority.

The Greek word translated "allow" *(epitrepō)* is always used in the New Testament to speak of permitting someone to do what they want. Paul's choice of words implies that some women in Ephesus desired to teach and have authority. In today's church, as in Ephesus, some women are dissatisfied with their God-given role. They want a prominent position, including the opportunity to exercise authority over men. There is only one biblical way to handle that situation for the good of everyone concerned, and that is to do what Paul did — honestly and directly: forbid women from taking the authoritative pastor-teacher role in the church.

Paul's use of the present infinitive *didaskein* translated "to teach" could better be translated "to be a teacher." By using the present infinitive instead of the aorist, Paul does not forbid women to teach under any circumstances, but to fill the office of a teacher.

Paul also forbids women from exercising "authority over a man." The Greek word translated "exercise authority over" *(authentein)* appears only here in the New Testament. Some have attempted to evade the force of Paul's prohibition by arguing that *authentein* refers to abusive or destructive authority. Women, according to this view, can both teach and exercise authority over men so long as it is not abusive or destructive (Aida Besançon Spencer, *Beyond the Curse* [Peabody, Mass.: Hendrickson, 1989], 87–88). Others claim it carries the idea of "author" or "originator," thus Paul is actually saying, "I do not allow a woman to teach or proclaim herself author of man" (R.C. Kroeger and C.C. Kroeger, *I Suffer Not a Woman* [Grand Rapids: Baker, 1992], 192). In a study of the extrabiblical uses of *authentein,* however, Dr. George Knight concluded that the common meaning is "to have authority over" (The Pastoral Epistles: *A Commentary on the Greek Text* [Grand Rapids: Eerdmans, 1992], 141–42). Paul, then, forbids women from exercising any type of authority over men in the church, including teaching.

These instructions to Timothy echo what Paul earlier commanded the Corinthians, "As in all the churches of the saints, women should remain silent in the churches. They are not allowed to speak, but must be in submission, as the Law says . . . it is disgraceful for a woman to speak in church" (1 Cor. 14:33-35, NIV). Many claim Paul was addressing a cultural issue in Corinth – nothing that ought to concern our contemporary culture. But they fail to let the text speak for itself: "As in *all* the congregations of the saints, women should remain silent in the churches" (vv. 33-34, NIV, emphasis added). That isn't a cultural issue; it is God's standard for *all* churches.

The context implies that the silence Paul commands is not intended to preclude women from speaking at all but to prevent them from speaking in tongues and preaching in the church. As in Ephesus, certain women in Corinth were seeking prominent positions in the church, and particularly by abusing the gifts of speaking in tongues and prophesying. Yet these women, who joined in the chaotic self-expression Paul had been condemning, should not have been speaking at all. In God's order for the church, women should "subject themselves, just as the Law also says" (v. 34).

Women may be highly gifted teachers and leaders, but those gifts are not to be exercised over men in the services of the church. That is true not because women are spiritually inferior to men, but because God's law commands it. He has ordained order in His creation – an order that reflects His own nature and therefore should be reflected in His church. Anyone ignoring or rejecting God's order weakens the church and dishonors Him. Just as God's Spirit cannot be in control where there is confusion and chaos in the church, He cannot be in control when women usurp the role He has restricted to men.

Paul then says, "If they desire to learn anything, let them ask their own husbands at home" (v. 35). That implies certain women were disrupting the church service by asking questions. If they desired to learn, disrupting the church service was not the way to do it. Paul also implies that Christian husbands should be well taught in the Word. Frustration with Christian men, often including their own husbands, who do not responsibly fulfill their God-given leadership assignments, can tempt many women to go beyond their biblical roles. But God has established the proper order and relationship of male-female roles in the church, and they are not to be violated for any reason. For a woman to assume a man's role because he has neglected it merely compounds the problem. God has led women to do work that men have refused to do, but He does not lead them to accomplish that work through roles He has restricted to men.

That doesn't mean, however, that God never permits women to speak His truth in public:

• Paul spoke with various churches and synagogues during his missionary journeys, answering questions from women as well as men (cf. Acts 17:2-4). I see nothing wrong with a woman asking questions or sharing what the Spirit of God has taught her out of the Word during informal Bible study and fellowship. In fact, when we have a question-and-answer session in our church, I believe it's proper for anyone to ask a question—because that's the specified order of the time. But the ordinary worship service of the church is never to be interrupted and usurped by anyone's questions. I also think there is a time and place for women to publicly offer a testimony of praise to the Lord.

• I thank God for the many faithful women who serve on the mission field in a variety of public ways, but refrain from leading the church. If there was ever a need for leadership on the mission field, it was in Paul's day. He could have compromised by using women in leadership roles, but he didn't. When a shortage of men exists on the mission field, don't violate biblical principles but instead ask the Lord of the harvest to send more laborers (Matt. 9:38).

Elisabeth Elliot, after the murder of her husband and several other missionaries in Ecuador, was the only missionary left who could speak the language of the Auca Indians. Rather than violate the Word of God, she taught one of the Auca men the sermon each week, and he then preached it to the church until male leaders could be found.

• Women can proclaim the Word of God except when the church meets for corporate worship. The Old Testament says, "The women who proclaim the good tidings are a great host" (Ps. 68:11). The New Testament gives examples of Mary, Anna, and Priscilla declaring God's truth to men and women (Luke 1:46-55; 2:36-38; Acts 18:24-26).

• Women can pray in public. Acts 1:13-14 describes a prayer meeting where women and men, including Jesus' apostles, were present. But during an official meeting of the church, leading in prayer, as we've already seen, is a role ordained for men (1 Tim. 2:8).

Appropriate times abound for men and women to share equally in exchanging questions and insights. But when the church comes together as a body to worship God, His standards are clear: the role of leadership is reserved for men.

The Order of Creation

A popular view today is that woman's subordinate role is a result of the Fall. Since God reversed the effects of the curse through Christ, some argue, He abolished differing male and female roles. Paul, however, grounds woman's subordinate role in the order of Creation, not in the Fall: "For it was Adam who was first created, and then Eve" (1 Tim. 2:13). As we noted in chapter 1, Eve was created after Adam to be his helper (Gen. 2:18) — she was designed to follow his lead, live on his provisions, and find safety in his strength. Such tendencies were from that point on built into all women, but with the Fall came conflict.

Nor was Paul's teaching prompted by some cultural situation at Ephesus and hence not applicable today, as others argue. He also taught this same truth to the Corinthians (1 Cor. 11:8-9).

Paul does not derive woman's role from the Fall; he uses that event as further corroboration. He points out that "it was not Adam who was deceived, but the woman being quite deceived, fell into transgression" (1 Tim. 2:14).

We usually connect the Fall with Adam since Romans 5:12-21 speaks repeatedly of the one man (Adam) who ushered sin and death into the world. Although he was not deceived by Satan, as was Eve, Adam still chose to disobey God. As the head of their relationship, he bore ultimate responsibility. But we must keep in mind that he didn't actually fall first — Eve did (Gen. 3:1-6). When Eve abandoned the protection of Adam's leadership and attempted to deal independently with the enemy, she was deceived.

By being so easily deceived, Eve revealed her inability to lead effectively. She had met more than her match in Satan. The Greek word translated "deceived" in 1 Timothy 2:14 is a particularly strong term: It refers to being thoroughly deceived. When a woman leaves the shelter of her protector, she exposes a certain amount of vulnerability.

The Fall resulted not only from direct disobedience of God's command, but also from a violation of the divinely appointed role of the sexes. Eve acted independently and assumed the role of leadership; Adam abdicated his leadership and followed Eve's lead. That does not mean Adam was less culpable than Eve, or that she was more defective — both were wrong. We're all vulnerable in different ways.

Christians affirm the leadership of men in the church because it is established by Creation and confirmed by the Fall. The headship of man, then, was part of God's design from the beginning. The tragic experience of the Fall confirmed the wisdom of that design. No daughter of Eve should follow her path and enter the forbidden territory of rulership intended for men.

THE CONTRIBUTION OF WOMEN

God designed life to revolve around relationships, and within those relationships are differing roles. In our society, unfortunately, more emphasis is placed on individuality than on relationships. People seek to satisfy themselves and focus on their rights rather than on how they can best serve others. When men and women refuse to accept their God-ordained roles in the church, family, and community, they undermine the foundational design of God for those institutions and all the relationships involved. The stability of society is at stake. If there's one thing all the social experiments we noted have proved, it is that.

Women are *not* inferior to men; they simply have a different role. Many people believe the only place of power and influence in society is in a leadership position, assuming it is more fulfilling to lead than to follow. But people in nonleadership roles can be very influential. Besides, a leader carries a heavy load of responsibility that is not always desirable (James 3:1). The notion that the greatest experience in life is to be on top of the pile and control everything is an illusion. As Dr. Tannen, Maggie Gallagher, and Marilyn Quayle implied in our introduction, it is women who suffer most from that misperception. Society, in turn, suffers from not receiving the benefit of a woman's best effort if she has been misdirected to pursue that which is not her strength.

Through Bearing Children

First Timothy 2:15 speaks somewhat cryptically of the influence women have by pursuing their strengths: "But women shall be preserved through the bearing of children if they continue in faith and love and sanctity with self-restraint." The context helps our understanding: Verse 14 speaks of women being in sin; verse 15, of women being saved. Paul was making clever use of the literary device of contrast.

"Preserved" is from *sōzō*, the common New Testament word for salvation. Paul obviously does not intend to teach that women are saved from sin "through the bearing of children." That would contradict the New Testament's teaching that salvation is by faith alone. The future tense and the use of the plural pronoun "they" indicate that he was not referring to Eve. Those considerations plus the lack of any connection to the context show Paul was not referring to Mary the mother of Jesus either.

Paul does teach that although a woman precipitated the Fall, women are preserved from that stigma through childbearing. A woman led the human race into sin, yet women benefit mankind by replenishing it. Beyond that, they have the opportunity to lead the race to godliness through their influence on their children. Far from being second-class citizens, women have the primary responsibility for rearing godly children.

A mother's virtue has a profound impact on the life of her children. Mothers usually spend far more time with their children than do their fathers, and thus have the greater influence. For women to fulfill their calling to raise a godly seed, they must "continue in faith and love and sanctity with self-restraint." To raise godly children, a woman must be godly herself.

Obviously God doesn't want all women to be mothers. Some He doesn't even want married since He has given them the gift of singleness (1 Cor. 7). Others He allows to be childless for His own purposes. But as a general rule, motherhood is the greatest contribution a woman can make to the human race. The pain of childbearing was the punishment for the first sin, but the bearing of children delivers women from the stigma of that sin.

Through Using Spiritual Gifts
Although Paul

> excludes women from any activity involving the *leadership* of men . . . he encourages women in many forms of *ministry*. . . . The whole chapter 16 in Romans is an eye-opener to those who have thought of Paul as a woman hater! A third of those he commends are women. . . . They bear the title "fellow worker," *colleagues* of Paul (as were Euodia and Syntyche in Philippians 4:2), which means they shared in his mission of evangelism and church-planting (J. David Pawson, *Leadership Is Male,* [Nashville: Thomas Nelson, 1990], 89–90, emphasis in original).

The Bible teaches that each Christian, at the moment of salvation, receives complementary spiritual gifts from God that enable the church to function smoothly (Rom. 12:3-14;

1 Cor. 12:4-30; Eph. 4:1-13). The permanent edifying gifts
come in two categories: speaking gifts and serving gifts
(1 Peter 4:10-11). Those gifted in speaking excel in one or
more of the following: teaching, wisdom (giving practical advice), knowledge (imparting scholarly information), exhorta-
tion, and leadership. Those gifted in serving have one or
more of these strengths: showing mercy, having strong faith
(especially manifested in prayer), giving (meeting needs), discerning truth from error, helping (doing nonglorious essen-
tials), and administrating or organizing.

Spiritual gifts — as opposed to church offices — are not gender defined in Scripture. An important challenge for men in
church leadership is to encourage and provide opportunities
for both men and women to minister to the body of Christ in
ways that genuinely employ their spiritual gifts, whether pre-
dominantly speaking or serving.

God does see fit to gift some women with leadership and
teaching abilities. They can and do use those gifts in situations apart from the worship service of the church — a wom-
en's Bible study, fellowship group, prayer meeting, or class
situation, for example. There's plenty of opportunity for
women to exercise their gifts and other abilities in a manner
consistent with God's design.

Our text in 1 Timothy 2, far from being an insult to a
woman's intelligence, instead provides practical direction on
how she can best apply her skills. And one of those skills may
be teaching.

Under the inspiration of the Holy Spirit, Paul teaches wom-
en to accept their God-given role. They must not seek the
leadership role in the church. How tragic that so many wom-
en feel their lives are unfulfilled because they can't function
in the same role as men! For most women, their greatest
impact on society is through raising godly children. If a woman is godly and if God chooses to give her children whom she
raises in the "discipline and instruction of the Lord" (Eph.
6:4), she will have a profound influence on a new generation.
Men have the outward, overt leadership by God's design, but
women can have just as great an influence indirectly.

CHAPTER 8

The Character of Service

Many years ago during my early days at Grace Community Church, *Moody Monthly* decided to publish an article about our church. At the time we met in a smaller building and were bursting at the seams with people. After interviewing different people, the writer decided to entitle his article, "The Church with Nine Hundred Ministers." He did so because 900 people attended our church and everyone was actively serving. We didn't have many formal programs, but each person was ministering his or her gifts. People were continually calling the church and asking how they could help. They were available to visit someone in the hospital, help in our nursery, clean our buildings, evangelize, or teach a class. People were constantly sharing with each other how God was blessing their ministry, giving God the glory for all that was happening. That's the way God designed the church: to consist of people ready to serve.

Several words in the Greek language express the attitude

of a servant. In 1 Corinthians 4:1 Paul used one that best conveyed the idea of a lowly servant: "Let a man regard us in this manner, as servants [Gk., *hupēretēs*, 'an under rower'] of Christ." In those days, large wooden three-tiered ships were propelled by slaves chained to their oars in the hull. The slaves on the lowest tier were called "under rowers." Paul and his coworkers didn't want to be exalted; they wanted to be known as third-level galley slaves who pulled their oars.

Many people want to be hotshots, but God wants people who will be obedient servants. In verse 2 Paul says, "It is required of stewards that one be found trustworthy." God doesn't want a person to come up with a clever new way to pull his oar and shear off everyone else's oars in the process! He wants faithful rowers who see themselves as willing servants.

I see the feminist debate in this light. Instead of exemplifying the humble attitude expressed by Paul, many want women to acquire equal access to leadership roles in the church — roles that God has designed only for men. But they fail to take into account God's overall design for the order and function of His church.

In Romans 12:4-5 Paul describes that design, using the human body as an analogy: "As we have many members in one body and all members do not have the same function, so we, who are many, are one body in Christ, and individually members one of another." While the human body has many parts — a head, eyes, nose, mouth, ears, teeth, arms, legs, fingers, toes, and internal organs — they all don't have the same function. That analogy beautifully illustrates the relationship of individual believers to the entire body of Christ. We constitute one body, yet we have different roles that complement one another.

Like a human body whose parts work together, believers form a spiritual body, sharing common life, gifts, ministry, resources, joy, and sorrow. That expresses our unity; yet at the same time we are all diverse. If one part of your body isn't functioning, you've got a problem — you might even have to be hospitalized. Every part must work together for the body as a whole to work properly. Likewise, everyone in the church must work together or the entire church suffers. Because each believer has something unique to offer, if we don't do what we are gifted and designed to do, we impair the body of Christ.

Only as each member serves in some capacity does the church function as it should. While a small percentage of men are called to lead the church, the rest of the congregation, both men and women alike, must serve. A common Greek word gives us a sense of the various levels at which believers can serve.

LEVELS OF SERVICE

Diakonos ("servant") and the related terms *diakoneō* ("to serve"), and *diakonia* ("service") appear approximately 100 times in the New Testament. The original meaning of this word group referred to performing menial tasks such as waiting on tables. That meaning gradually broadened until it included any kind of service.

The meaning of *diakonos* is primarily general, with the exception of its uses in 1 Timothy 3 and Philippians 1:1. Only in those two cases did the translators of most versions of the Bible transliterate it *deacon,* as if to set it apart specifically to refer to a group of select people called to serve the church. In every other occurrence, the New Testament writers used *diakonos, diakoneō,* and *diakonia* the same way we use *servant, serve,* and *service.*

The root idea of serving food comes across in John 2:5, where *diakonos* is used of the waiters at a wedding. *Diakoneō* is used in the same sense in Luke 4:39, where Peter's mother-in-law served a meal.

As the Gospel and epistle writers adapted the term, they used these words in a general sense for all types of spiritual service. In John 12:26, Jesus equated following Him with serving Him. Anything we do in obedience to Him is spiritual service—and ought to be the major emphasis of our lives. In that sense all Christians are deacons, for all are to actively serve Christ. The church is not made up of three levels: elders who lead, deacons who serve, and everyone else, who make up the audience. There are no spectators in the church—

all are called into the service of Christ.

That is Paul's point in 1 Corinthians 12:5, where he writes that "there are varieties of ministries." Every Christian is to be involved in some form of spiritual service. Leaders, through both teaching and modeling, are to equip believers to perform that service (Eph. 4:12).

Diakonos, diakonia, and *diakoneō* are also used in a second, more specific sense. The list of spiritual gifts in Romans 12:6-8 includes service. Those who have that gift are specially equipped, though they may not hold the office of deacon. Stephanas and his family were so gifted: "They have devoted themselves for ministry [*diakonia*] to the saints" (1 Cor. 16:15).

The third use of this word group refers to the office of deacon. Deacons serve in an official capacity as servants of the church. We could just as easily call them servants.

Although they are servants, deacons are not to do all the work—they are to model spiritual service for the body. In that sense they stand alongside the elders. While elders have been given authority through their responsibility in teaching God's Word, deacons are equal to elders in every other respect. In implementing what the elders teach, deacons seek to raise the congregation to the highest level of spiritual virtue, not to set themselves apart as especially pious people whom the congregation can never expect to imitate.

When Paul wrote 1 Timothy the church had grown and developed to the point where there was a need for deacons to function as models of spiritual virtue and service. To ensure that those elevated to that office were worthy, Paul lists several qualifications they must meet. As with elders, these qualifications relate to their spiritual character, not their function. In fact, no specifics are given in Scripture as to the duties of deacons. They were to carry out whatever tasks were assigned to them by the elders.

THE QUALIFICATIONS FOR MALE DEACONS
Paul writes,

> Deacons likewise must be men of dignity, not double-tongued, or addicted to much wine or fond of sordid

gain, but holding to the mystery of the faith with a clear conscience. And let these also first be tested; then let them serve as deacons if they are beyond reproach. . . . Let deacons be husbands of only one wife, and good managers of their children and their own households (1 Tim. 3:8-10, 12).

"Likewise" introduces a new category within the overall topic of church leaders. Having discussed elders in 3:1-7, Paul now turns to deacons. He gives five areas in which a deacon must be qualified.

Personal Character
Serious
The Greek word translated "dignity" (*semnos*) means "serious," and conveys the idea of being serious in mind as well as in character. *Semnos* comes from the root verb *sebōmai*, which means "to venerate" or "to worship." Those characterized by it have a majestic quality about them that commands the respect of others. A synonym of *semnos* is *hieroprepēs*, which means "to act like a sacred person." A deacon must not be silly or flippant, making light of serious matters.

Verbal Honesty
A deacon must not be "double-tongued." Some think that refers to a gossip, a person who has, so to speak, not one but two tongues going. It seems best, however, to interpret it as a prohibition against saying one thing to one person and another thing to someone else to further one's personal agenda. Because deacons are privy to certain private matters and grave spiritual issues, they need to speak with integrity. The church must place a high premium on verbal honesty and integrity among spiritual leaders. A man who tells different stories to different people will quickly lose their confidence.

Not Preoccupied with Alcohol
Paul forbids deacons from being "addicted to much wine." The Greek word translated "addicted to" means "to turn

one's mind to," or "to occupy oneself with." The present active participle indicates this is to be the deacon's habitual practice. He is not to be preoccupied with drink, nor to allow it to influence his life.

Some of you may wonder why the Lord did not require total abstinence. As Homer A. Kent, Jr. points out, however,

> It is extremely difficult for the twentieth-century American to understand and appreciate the society of Paul's day. The fact that deacons were not told to become total abstainers, but rather to be temperate, does not mean that Christians today can use liquor in moderate amounts. The wine employed for the common beverage was very largely water. The social stigma and the tremendous social evils that accompany drinking today did not attach themselves to the use of wine as the common beverage in the homes of Paul's day. Nevertheless, as the church grew and the Christian consciousness and conscience developed, the dangers of drinking came to be more clearly seen. The principle laid down elsewhere by Paul that Christians should not do anything to cause a brother to stumble came to be applied to the use of wine. Raymond states it this way:

> > If an individual by drinking wine either causes others to err through his example or abets a social evil which causes others to succumb to its temptations, then in the interests of Christian love he ought to forego the temporary pleasures of drinking in the interests of heavenly treasures (Irwin Woodworth Raymond, *The Teaching of the Early Church on the Use of Wine and Strong Drink* [New York: Columbia U., 1927], 88).

> Certainly in present-day America, the use of wine by a Christian would abet a recognized social evil, and would set a most dangerous example for the young and the weak. To us, Paul would undoubtedly say, "No wine at all" (*The Pastoral Epistles* [Chicago: Moody, 1982], 133).

Free from Greed
In New Testament times those who served in the church were often involved in distributing money to widows, orphans, and others in need. Since banks and audit firms did not exist in those days, every transaction involved cash. The people who handled the money actually carried it in a little purse on their belt. The temptation was always present to steal from those funds, as did Judas (John 12:4-6). It was essential, then, that deacons be free from the love of money.

Spiritual Life

Paul also says that deacons ought to be "holding to the mystery of the faith with a clear conscience." The Greek word translated "mystery" refers to something that was once hidden but now revealed. The "mystery of the faith" is the New Testament revelation of God's redemptive truth, which was not fully revealed in the Old Testament. It encompasses the mystery of the incarnation of Christ (1 Tim. 3:16), of the indwelling of Christ in believers (Col. 1:26-27), of the unity of Jews and Gentiles in Christ (Eph. 1:9; 3:4-6), of the saving Gospel (Col. 4:3), of lawlessness (2 Thes. 2:7), and of the rapture of the church (1 Cor. 15:51-52).

The deacon's spiritual character must begin with an affirmation of New Testament doctrine. He holds to the mystery of *"the* faith," which simply refers to the content of Christian truth. And he must hold to it "with a clear conscience," that is, a conscience that does not accuse him. It is not enough merely to believe the truth (cf. James 2:19); you must also live it. And the stronger your theological and biblical knowledge, the stronger your conscience. Every deacon (and every Christian) should strive to be able to say with Paul, "For our proud confidence is this, the testimony of our conscience, that in holiness and godly sincerity, not in fleshly wisdom but in the grace of God, we have conducted ourselves in the world, and especially toward you" (2 Cor. 1:12).

Spiritual Service

Paul next gives a specific prerequisite: "Let these also first be tested; then let them serve as deacons" (1 Tim. 3:10).

This is an imperative. The Greek verb *(dokimazō)* translated "be tested" is in the present passive tense, which implies an ongoing test, not a single test or probationary period.

Then Paul issues another imperative: "Let them serve as deacons." Each deacon's service to Christ is to be continually tested in an ongoing general assessment by the church.

Moral Purity

Deacons, no less than elders, must be "beyond reproach." While deacons differ in function from elders in that elders are the primary teachers of the church, the spiritual requirements for both offices are the same. Hence, all the requirements for elders (except being able to teach) apply equally to deacons. They sum up what it means to be beyond reproach. Deacons must not have any blot on their lives, nothing for which they could be accused and disqualified.

That's important because some deacons may one day become pastors or elders. Their experience in implementing the teaching of the pastors and elders is invaluable as preparation for a leadership role. By meeting the personal needs of the flock, deacons acquire firsthand knowledge of the special and specific requirements of people in the congregation.

Paul reiterates one key element from the qualifications given for elders. Deacons too must "be husbands of only one wife." They must not be unfaithful to their wives either in their deeds, or in their hearts. As with elders, the issue is moral character, not marital status.

Home Life

Deacons, like elders, must prove their leadership abilities in the home. They are to be "good managers of their children" and their money, possessions, and everything associated with "their own households." They prove their leadership abilities by how capably they handle situations in their home.

THE QUALIFICATIONS FOR FEMALE DEACONS

In 1 Timothy 3:11 Paul refers to a separate group of deacons: "Women must likewise be dignified, not malicious gossips, but temperate, faithful in all things." Several factors point toward Paul's referring to a separate order of women deacons here and not deacons' wives. First, the use of "likewise" (cf. 2:9; 3:8; Titus 2:3, 6) argues strongly for seeing a third group here in addition to elders and deacons. Second, there is no possessive pronoun or definite article connecting these women with deacons. Third, since Paul gave no qualifications for elders' wives, why would he do so for deacons' wives? Fourth, Paul did not use the word "deaconesses" because there was no such word in the Greek language. Phoebe is called a deacon in Romans 16:1 because there's no feminine form of *diakonos*. The only other word Paul could have used would have been *diakonos*, but we would not have known that he was referring to women. Using the term "women" (Gk., *gunaikeios*) was the only way Paul could distinguish them from the male deacons. Finally, their qualifications parallel those of the male deacons. Clearly Paul introduced another category of deacons: what we have come to know as deaconesses. I prefer to call them women deacons because that maintains the New Testament terminology.

Dignified
Paul uses the same word here that he used in verse 8 to describe male deacons. Female deacons, like their male counterparts, must lead serious lives. People should hold them in awe because of their spiritual devotion.

Not Malicious Gossips
The Greek word translated "malicious gossips" *(diabolos)* means "slanderer." It is often used to describe Satan, and is translated "devil" (cf. Matt. 4:1). Women deacons must control their tongues. Just as men deacons are not to be "double-tongued" (1 Tim. 3:8), women deacons should never betray a confidence or slander anyone.

Temperate
The same Greek word was used of elders in verse 2, and it parallels the third qualification of deacons in verse 8 — "not given to much wine." Women deacons are to be sober and

sensible in their judgments. That's impossible if they're not sober physically.

Trustworthy
Finally, women deacons must be "faithful in all things." They must be absolutely trustworthy. That qualification parallels the requirement that a male deacon not be "fond of sordid gain" (v. 8). Like male deacons, women deacons handled money while performing their duties. Those who were unfaithful could not be trusted.

THE REWARDS OF SERVICE
Paul closes his treatment of men and women deacons with a promise: "For those who have served well as deacons obtain for themselves a high standing and great confidence in the faith that is in Christ Jesus" (v. 13). Two rewards await "those who have served well as deacons."

First, they "obtain for themselves a high standing." The Greek word translated "standing" literally refers to a step. Here it is used metaphorically to speak of those who are a step above everyone else. In our vernacular, we might say they are put on a pedestal. While that might seem sinful, it's not if the person didn't seek that honor. Those who serve humbly will be exalted by God (James 4:10; 1 Peter 5:6), and by men. If you serve well as a deacon, the people who witness your faithful service will respect and honor you. That doesn't mean they'll give you some earthly award, but you will have gained their spiritual respect. That is the key to being a spiritual example, since only respected people are emulated.

A second reward is "great confidence in the faith that is in Christ Jesus." The Greek word translated "confidence" is often used of boldness of speech. Success breeds confidence and assurance. If you serve God well, you will see His power and grace at work in your life, and that will energize you for even greater service.

Men and women deacons, no less than elders, are vital to a healthy church. The church must be careful to choose fully qualified men and women for these important roles.

THE CHARACTERISTICS OF A
HEALTHY CONGREGATION

Don't think Paul thought only of qualifications for the church offices of elders and deacons. On the contrary, the church as a whole was always a concern of his—especially its spiritual health and vitality. That was why he wrote his epistle to Titus, so he "might set in order what remains, and appoint elders in every city" (Titus 1:5). Just as he did for Timothy, Paul left Titus with a list of qualifications for the type of men he was to choose to lead the churches in Crete (vv. 6-9).

Unlike his instructions for Timothy, however, Paul left no list for the qualifications of deacons. Since these churches were quite young, there may not have been a need for the specific office of deacon. In addition, since the leadership had not yet been selected to lead the various congregations, it's likely Paul would have wanted those leaders to be involved in choosing those who were qualified to serve in an official capacity. Yet he did leave a list of qualifications for the entire congregation, broken down by age group and gender. And this list is intended to reflect what Paul wanted Titus to focus on with respect to the people: "Speak the things which are fitting for sound doctrine" (2:1). The Greek word translated "sound" gives us the English word "hygiene," and it basically means "healthy." God is concerned that His church be characterized by sound, healthy teaching that will result in sound, healthy living. The following characteristics reveal the type of people that populate such a church.

Older Men

Paul first gave instructions for the older men in the congregation. He used the same term translated "older men" in Philemon 9 in referring to himself as "Paul the aged," and he was in his sixties at that time. These older men "are to be temperate, dignified, sensible, sound in faith, in love, in perseverance" (Titus 2:2). Men who have walked with Christ for a long time have accumulated a wealth of spiritual experience, enabling them to be examples to the young. There's no value in being old if you're not godly, however, so the Apostle Paul lays down three specific characteristics followed by three virtues that ought to be manifest by the older men.

Temperate
This characteristic ought to be quite familiar to you by now. It is the same one Paul used in reference to elders (1 Tim. 3:2) and women deacons (v. 11), and which parallels the requirement that male deacons not be addicted to much wine (vv. 2, 8). While the word literally means "unmixed with wine," metaphorically it means "moderate" or "not indulgent." Godly older believers are not given to excess. They have learned the high cost that accompanies a self-indulgent lifestyle. When most men reach this age in life, they know what has real value. Such a wise assessment of priorities needs to be passed down to the next generation.

Dignified
Older men also are to be "dignified." That is the same characteristic that is to be true of both men and women deacons (vv. 8, 11). Older godly men hold a serious attitude toward life. That doesn't mean they're gloomy, but neither are they frivolous or flippant. They've experienced too much to be trivial. In most cases they've buried their parents, some have witnessed the deaths of sisters or brothers, some have lost their life partner. They may have even lost some of their children through rebellion or even death.

They see life the way it really is. When they laugh, they laugh at what is truly laughable, not what is tragic. They enjoy what is truly enjoyable—a beautiful day, a precious child, and meaningful relationships.

Sensible
Older men also ought to be sensible. As we noted regarding elders, this is the resulting characteristic of someone who is temperate. That means they are self-disciplined, operating with discretion and discernment. They have learned how to control their instincts and passions. As Paul said in Romans 12:3, they "think so as to have sound judgment."

The qualities of being temperate, dignified, and sensible replace the more unfortunate qualities of youth: recklessness, impetuosity, thoughtlessness, and instability.

Sound in Faith
As we discovered, "sound" means "healthy." That means
their faith in God is unwavering. Through the years they
have realized God can be trusted, observing His ongoing
faithfulness. As a result they don't doubt or question His
good intention nor lose confidence in His plan. Neither do
they doubt the truth of Scripture or question the power of the
Holy Spirit. They know the Gospel can save. That kind of
mature faith upholds the church because it gives us a faith to
emulate.

Sound in Love
A godly older man also has a healthy love not only of God but
others as well. Here is a man who loves by bearing one
another's burdens (Gal. 6:2). He loves sacrificially. Through
the years he has learned what to love and what not to love.
He loves when his love is not returned, when it is rejected,
and even when it isn't deserved. His love is "patient . . . kind,
and is not jealous; [his] love does not brag and is not arrogant, does not act unbecomingly; it does not seek its own, is
not provoked, does not take into account a wrong suffered,
does not rejoice in unrighteousness, but rejoices with the
truth; bears all things, believes all things, hopes all things,
endures all things. Love never fails" (1 Cor. 13:4-8). He loves
with his will, not his feelings.

Sound in Perseverance
A godly older man is the model of patience because he has
endured many trials. In spite of disappointment, unfulfilled
aspirations, physical weakness, and growing loneliness, he
never loses heart. The godly man becomes tempered like
steel. His body is weaker but his spirit is stronger, enabling
him to endure to the very end.

Older Women
Next Paul suggests several qualities that should mark another group in the church: "Older women likewise are to be

reverent in their behavior, not malicious gossips, nor en-
slaved to much wine, teaching what is good" (Titus 2:3).

Reverent

The Greek word translated "reverent" is used only here in
the Bible, and it conveys the idea of priestlike. Older women
are to be holy. Their sacred character should influence every
aspect of their lives. The widow Anna, who served night and
day in the temple, is an example of a godly woman who was
priestlike in her behavior (Luke 2:36-38).

Not Malicious Gossips

This is the same characteristic that is to be true of women
deacons. Whereas men tend to be rough or violent in their
actions, women have a tendency to be rough or violent in
their words. Older women who find themselves with time on
their hands can be tempted to allow their conversations to
lead to gossip, criticism, and slander.

Not Enslaved to Much Wine

This third characteristic recalls similar prohibitions required
of elders and men and women deacons. Here the emphasis is
on the enslaving aspect of strong drink. Older women are not
to be drunkards. Apparently in Crete older women turned to
stimulants to refresh their weary bodies and tired minds.
Perhaps in the pain and maybe even in the loneliness of their
old age, older women tended to dull their senses. But Paul
requires godly women to be in full command of their faculties
for God's holy purposes.

Teaching What Is Good

Instead of being occupied with gossiping or drinking, older
women need to be busy "teaching what is good" — what is
noble and excellent — to the younger women. The implication
is that they've already taught their children, who have since
left home. Now they have the opportunity to teach the younger generation of women in the church.

As we noted in the previous chapter, their instruction is
not to occur in the worship service, but in informal settings,

such as one on one, small groups, or women's Bible studies. And their instruction is both by word and example. I fear for the future of the church if godly women don't teach the next generation because many young women today were not raised under a biblical family model. That's a challenge for the older women in the church.

In teaching what is good they "encourage the young women" (Titus 2:4). The Greek word translated "encourage" is *sōphronizō,* which essentially means, "to train someone in self-control." You will note the similarity of this form to characteristics of elders, "prudent" (1 Tim. 3:2), and older men, "sensible" (Titus 2:2). Older women are to train the younger women to learn the art of self-restraint. This training process requires that you older women be committed to being responsible, confrontive, and affirming in an ongoing relationship with a younger woman.

Younger Women

The older women are to train the younger women "to love their husbands, to love their children, to be sensible, pure, workers at home, kind, being subject to their own husbands" (vv. 4-5). In our culture, that is the exact opposite of what they are being taught. Women today are encouraged to love whomever they want, to farm out their children to someone else's care and influence, and not to worry about being sensible or pure, but to do whatever pleases them in fulfilling their desires.

"Younger women" refers to those women who are able to bear children or are still rearing children. Since women can bear children well into their forties and the main duties of raising a child last for about twenty years, a woman under sixty could be considered young in the biblical sense (1 Tim. 5:9). What qualities ought to characterize her life?

Love Their Husbands
One word in the Greek text, *philandros,* is translated "love their husbands." Paul used the same terms to describe godly widows (1 Tim. 5:9). It means to be a one-man woman, totally devoted to one's husband.

I've had women tell me that their husbands are no longer lovable. But having that attitude is disobedience to the clear Word of God. To help your attitude, keep in mind that loving your husband doesn't mean you'll always feel the rush of emotion that characterized your love at the beginning of your relationship. A recent cover story in *Time* magazine explained that those initial feelings change in a couple of years because of chemical changes and mellow into something deeper (Paul Gray, "What Is Love?" [15 Feb. 1993]:47–51). Marriage is a contented commitment that goes beyond feelings to a devotedness—to a level of friendship that is deep and satisfying.

If you don't love your husband, you need to train yourself to love him. Serve him kindly and graciously day by day and soon you will make such a great investment in him, you will say to yourself, *I've put too much of myself into this guy not to love him!* It is a sin to disobey this command.

A Lover of Children

This characteristic is also one word in the Greek text, *philoteknos,* and it means to be a lover of children. As we saw from our study of 1 Timothy 2:15, that is a woman's highest calling. Obviously God doesn't want all women to be mothers or they would be. Those women who have no children mean a great deal to God's kingdom because He has given them freedom to serve in unique ways.

God wants women who are mothers to love their children, which involves making personal sacrifices for the benefit of their children. Remember, loving your children is not based on emotion. Rather, it is your responsibility to pour yourself into your child's life so that he or she grows up to love Christ.

Sensible

Young women are to be taught to be sensible, a required characteristic of elders (1 Tim. 3:2) and older men (Titus 2:2). It refers to using common sense and making sound judgments. Those things are learned best by example, and that's where the older women can have such an influence.

Pure
Young women are to be morally pure, virtuous, and sexually faithful to their husbands. They are to be devoted to that one man in body and spirit.

Worker at Home
Titus 2:5 also says young women are to be "workers at home." Since we examined this quality in depth in chapter 6, I'll just reiterate this one thought: a woman's responsibility is in the home because it is the place where she can have the greatest impact on the world by raising godly men and women.

Kind
A young woman ought to be characterized by being gentle, tender-hearted, and merciful toward others.

Subject to Their Own Husbands
This echoes Paul's instruction in Ephesians 5:22. A godly young woman understands God's created order and submits to it (cf. 1 Cor. 11:5).

Younger Men

Paul concludes his instruction for the various members of the congregation with a general word for all the young men, and then with some specific encouragement for Titus: "Likewise, urge the young men to be sensible; in all things show yourself to be an example of good deeds, with purity in doctrine, dignified, sound in speech which is beyond reproach" (Titus 2:6-8). Whereas Paul deals specifically with Titus in verses 7-8, I believe his instruction applies to all young men. As a young man himself, Titus had the unique opportunity to model these qualities for the other young men.

How young is young? As with the young women, this relates to anyone from around twenty to sixty—a time when men are basically virile, aggressive, and ambitious to one degree or another. While those are some of the greatest years in life, they can also be dangerous.

For one thing, young men are prone to laziness. A self-indulgent lifestyle, while innate in our depraved nature, is often programmed in men through the years. Laziness can be exacerbated in a variety of homes when men are young. Parents who lack self-discipline themselves, for example, produce children who never learn to set goals and work to meet them.

Those that favor child-centered approaches to parenting continually indulge their children, causing them to become dependent on others to serve them, rather than teaching them the value of service to others. In homes where parents are absent, children are left to themselves without any care, discipline, or work. When they can do what they please, young men will choose to do nothing beneficial, becoming victims of their own lethargy.

While laziness is certainly the most telling, young men must be protected from several other dangers. Turning young people loose from family accountability too soon is a serious problem. When they get out from under a strong influence and live without restraint and the resulting consequences of their behavior, they usually do not honor God or accomplish anything productive.

Another thing young men raised in our decadent culture are unfortunately familiar with is vice, and that produces attachment, not disgust. Victimized by the allurements of evil, young men are ignorant of the gradual decline in their moral sensitivity.

Another danger is secular education, with its resulting attacks on Christianity. An educational system that either ignores God or defines Him in human terms has a powerful influence over the minds of young men, who often look to their professors as mentors.

Youth is a time of unwarranted confidence and imagined invincibility—a time when immaturity rules. That's the time when temptation is at its strongest, when habits are formed that often bedevil men throughout their lifetimes. Yet the future of the church is dependent on young men growing up in such dangerous times. To combat these dangers, Paul instructs Titus and young men to cultivate certain godly qualities.

Sensible

Paul tells Titus to "urge the young men to be sensible; in all things" (vv. 6-7). We've seen Paul use this characteristic of elders, older men, and younger women. Young men need to develop self-control and balance, discernment and judgment (cf. 2 Tim. 2:22; 1 Peter 5:5). The phrase "in all things" at the beginning of Titus 2:7 fits better at the end of verse 6, for it stretches this matter of mental balance and self-mastery in the Christian life to an almost infinite level. Young men — so potentially volatile, impulsive, passionate, arrogant, and ambitious — need to become masters over every area in their lives.

Example of Good Deeds

Paul turns from the young men in general to encourage Titus to "show [himself] to be an example of good deeds." One of the most important qualities of a leader is the example he sets. Paul wanted Titus to be a model first of "good deeds." That refers to his inherent righteousness, nobility, and moral excellence. A godly young man is to model righteousness in everything he does. Young men, you'll begin to control your life when you understand God wants you committed to producing righteous, holy deeds.

Pure Motives

"With purity in doctrine" (v. 7) is how God wants those deeds accomplished. A better way to translate the Greek word is "uncorruptness." Titus and young men are to live in perfect accord with sound doctrine, and without defect. Young men must know the Word of God and live according to it. Psalm 119:9 says, "How can a young man keep his way pure? By keeping it according to Thy Word." Living in obedience to God's Word will keep you in line.

Dignified

At the end of Titus 2:7 Paul adds that Titus and young men are to be "dignified" — a characteristic that should also be true of men and women deacons and older men. That means young men are to be serious. Youth tends to be somewhat frivolous, particularly in our culture where entertainment has become an all-consuming passion. While that doesn't mean young men can't enjoy life, they should have a mature understanding of life, death, time, and eternity.

Sound Speech
Finally Paul encourages Titus to: "[Be] sound in speech which is beyond reproach." As we've seen, "sound" means "healthy" or "wholesome." In reference to one's words, Paul wrote, "Let your speech always be with grace, seasoned, as it were, with salt, so that you may know how you should respond to each person" (Col. 4:6). Young men, let what you say be worth saying. Make sure it edifies your hearers to the point that it is "beyond reproach" — that the only accusations which can be brought against it are shameful in the light of reason.

Solomon offers young men a thoughtful and fitting conclusion to this discussion of young men: "Rejoice, young man, during . . . the days of your young manhood. And follow the impulses of your heart and the desires of your eyes. Yet know that God will bring you to judgment for all these things. So, remove vexation from your heart and put away pain from your body, because childhood and the prime of life are fleeting" (Ecc. 11:9-10). While there's nothing wrong with enjoying your youth, one day we all will stand before God to give account for what we've done in those days. So Solomon encourages you young men to enjoy your youth, but make sure you remove anything from your life that will produce guilt and sorrow. How do you do that? By remembering "your Creator in the days of your youth" (12:1). In your old age you'll be able to enjoy wonderful memories of a well-spent youth.

Service to Christ is a wonderful opportunity that all who are a part of the household of God are privileged to have. Only as we seek to live holy lives will our service have any bearing on the health of the church or on our lost world.

CHAPTER 9

For the Sake
of the Kingdom

During World War II, missionaries Herb and Ruth Clingen
and their young son spent three years in a Japanese prison
camp in the Philippines. In his diary Herb recorded that their
captors murdered, tortured, and starved to death many of
their fellow prisoners. The camp commandant, Konishi, was
hated and feared. Herb writes,

> Konishi found an inventive way to abuse us even more.
> He *increased* the food ration but gave us *palay* —
> unhusked rice. Eating the rice with its razor-sharp outer
> shell would cause intestinal bleeding that would kill us
> in hours. We had no tools to remove the husks, and
> doing the job manually — by pounding the grain or rolling
> it with a heavy stick — consumed more calories than the
> rice would supply. It was a death sentence for all intern-
> ees (Herb and Ruth Clingen, "Song of Deliverance,"
> *Masterpiece* [Spring 1989], 12).

Before death could claim them, however, General Douglas MacArthur and his forces liberated them from captivity. That very day Konishi was preparing to slaughter the remaining prisoners. Years later Herb and Ruth "learned that Konishi had been found working as a groundskeeper at a Manila golf course. He was put on trial for his war crimes and hanged. Before his execution he professed conversion to Christianity, saying he had been deeply affected by the testimony of the Christian missionaries he had persecuted" ("Song of Deliverance," 13).

That wonderful story illustrates why God wants His people to live holy lives. Righteous living gives credence to the Gospel message we convey. We have no way of knowing who God will redeem or who may be watching intently how we live. But we can be sure that no one will be attracted to the Lord if our lives are indistinguishable from theirs.

That's why I'm so concerned when the church adopts worldly ideas. As I stated back in the first chapter, the church is in danger of following the world's lead when it comes to the roles of men and women. Succumbing to that type of compromise not only treads on God's specific design, but also ruins our opportunities for offering an alternative to those dissatisfied by the world's standards.

Despite the efforts of evangelical feminists to remain as biblically motivated as they claim they are, their support of leadership positions for women in the church actually undermines God's Word and what He wants to accomplish through them. They may win accolades from secular feminists for bucking "traditional" models established in the church throughout the centuries, but they fail where it really counts: in leading unredeemed souls to salvation in Christ. Human commendation may feed our pride, but it starves our humility and diverts us from leading sinners to repentance.

Holy, righteous lives are the backbone of the Gospel we preach. No torture Konishi tried could shake the faith and commitment of Herb and Ruth Clingen, and their testimony stuck with him, leading him to embrace their God. Konishi saw the reality of their faith when it really counted—when it was put to the test.

The Apostle Paul understood that. In the midst of a pagan society that did all it could to persecute Christians and discredit their faith, he continued to encourage the faithful. And that's the backdrop against which he wrote his epistles. Unfortunately the urgency of his exhortations are often lost on us as we live comfortably in a country that is still largely tolerant of Christianity.

Yet with the continual deterioration of godly values in this country, Paul's words are just as critical today as they've ever been. Over the last few chapters we've examined the character qualities that will characterize holy living in all God's children, whether they are men or women, young or old, married or unmarried, leaders or servants. His commands leave little doubt to the requirements of holy living. And we are well aware that if we obey them, God will bless our lives. Yet that wasn't Paul's purpose, for he had an even more imperative objective.

In the midst of Paul's instructions for Titus regarding the different gender and age-groups in the church, he gave three reasons for living holy lives, and they have nothing to do with how we'll benefit. As much as living a virtuous life will serve me and encourage fellow Christians, the compelling issue is what it will mean to unbelievers.

TO HONOR GOD'S WORD

After instructing Titus regarding older men and women and young women, he says they are to act in such a way so "that the Word of God may not be dishonored" (Titus 2:5). The Greek word translated "dishonored" literally means "blasphemed." We can't allow unbelievers to mock, ignore, or totally reject God's Word. Yet how we live will directly affect how people feel about it.

No matter what their station in life, Christian men and women who are not what they ought to be will give people reason to blaspheme God's Word. The world doesn't judge us by our theology; it judges us by our behavior. The validity of Scripture in the world's view is determined by how it affects us. If unbelievers see that our lives are truly transformed, separate and distinct from the world, they might conclude that Scripture is true, powerful, and life-changing.

The credibility of the Christian Gospel is inseparably linked to the integrity of the lives of those who proclaim it. That's why it is so devastating when well-known evangelists or Christian leaders are caught in some gross sin or immorality. How do you think unbelievers react when they see such hypocrisy? They laugh at it, thus blaspheming God's Word and short-circuiting any opportunity we have to tell them about its power to transform their lives. The impact of the lives of men and women who bear the Lord's name is vital to the credibility of the faith and the effectiveness of personal witness and preaching.

God called Israel to be a witness to Him among the nations of the world so they might glorify His name. But they failed and "the name of God is blasphemed among the Gentiles because of [them]" (Rom. 2:24). The nations attributed Israel's sins to the influence and impotence of their God and thus defiled God. That's why Jesus said, "Let your light shine before men in such a way that they may see your good works, and glorify your Father who is in heaven" (Matt. 5:16). You are the only Gospel unbelievers see, and you either make it believable or unbelievable.

In the context of Paul's instruction to Timothy regarding the qualifications for elders and deacons, he reiterated the importance of the church's responsibility to God's Word: "I write so that you may know how one ought to conduct himself in the household of God, which is the church of the living God, the pillar and support of the truth" (1 Tim. 3:15).

The imagery of the church as the pillar and support of God's truth would not have been lost on Timothy. The temple of the goddess Diana, one of the seven wonders of the ancient world, was located at Ephesus, and one of its features was its many pillars. Just as the foundation and pillars of the temple of Diana were a testimony to the error of pagan false religion, so the church is to be a testimony to God's truth. That is its mission and reason for existing.

"The truth" is the revealed truth of the Gospel, the content of the Christian faith. God has given His truth to us as a sacred treasure for His own glory and the good of men, and we must guard it as our most precious possession. Churches that abandon the truth destroy their only reason for existing and give unbelievers cause to blaspheme God. That's ultimately what is at stake in the way we live.

TO SILENCE THE OPPOSITION

Paul's second reason for living holy lives gives us the heart of what he wants to communicate: "That the opponent may be put to shame, having nothing bad to say about us" (Titus 2:8). The Greek word translated "put to shame" literally means "to blush," emphasizing the opponent's utter embarrassment over having no just criticism. Opponents of Christianity love to gloat when Christians cause a scandal. Don't you think some of the unbelievers in your sphere of influence would love to see you fail significantly so they can justify their unbelief? They don't want to see God transform your life — that would stand as a rebuke to their sinful lifestyles. But that's exactly what you want to do — you want to embarrass them when they criticize you because there is nothing for them to justifiably criticize.

The issue is evangelism. The proper strategy for our evangelization is not methodological. We reach the world through epitomizing virtue, godliness, holiness, and a purity of life that makes our faith and God's Word believable.

The Apostle Peter understood the way believers impact the godless world. He wrote, "Beloved, I urge you as aliens and strangers to abstain from fleshly lusts, which wage war against the soul. Keep your behavior excellent among the [pagans], so that in the thing in which they slander you as evildoers, they may on account of your good deeds, as they observe them, glorify God in the day of visitation" (1 Peter 2:11-12).

"The day of visitation" refers to a visit from God. In the Old Testament, God visited man for two reasons: blessing or judgment. The blessing was often some form of national deliverance from oppression (cf. Gen. 50:24; Jer. 27:22). In the New Testament, however, a visit from God specifically refers to redemption or salvation (cf. Luke 1:68).

Do you see how imperative it is that we live godly lives?

We want unbelievers to examine us. They come initially to criticize, but if our behavior is excellent, the criticism of some might turn to curiosity. And if that curiosity turns to conversion, they'll glorify God because of their salvation. Thus we've done our part in bringing God glory. You lead people to the credibility of Christianity and ultimately to conversion by the virtue of your life. So stay away from fleshly lusts and maintain excellent behavior.

TO MAKE THE GOSPEL ATTRACTIVE

Paul states his third reason for holy living in Titus 2:10, "That they may adorn the doctrine of God our Savior in every respect." "Adorn" is from the Greek word *kosmeō* and refers to making something beautiful.

What is our primary message to this world about God? Do we want the world to know that God is omnipotent? Omniscient? Omnipresent? Immutable? Sovereign? Eternal? The Creator and the Sustainer of the universe? Yes, we do. But by far the main attribute of God we want the unsaved to understand is that He is a Savior.

But how will we ever make the good news about God as Savior beautiful in every respect if we don't look like we've been saved? If I tell you about a great restaurant I've been eating at for fifteen years and that I'll eat there till I die, and a few days later I'm diagnosed with a terminal illness due to food poisoning, you're going to question the advisability of eating at such a place. Commending something that doesn't have a positive impact in my life is futile. The only way I can make the Gospel message beautiful or desirable is to demonstrate that I've been saved. But saved from what?

The fact that we are to make the Gospel attractive to unbelievers presupposes that they find their lives unattractive. But what makes unbelievers realize they have something wrong with them? Paul identified the source when he wrote the Ephesians to

walk as children of light (for the fruit of light consists in all goodness and righteousness and truth), trying to learn what is pleasing to the Lord. And do not participate in the unfruitful deeds of darkness, but instead even expose them; for it is disgraceful even to speak of the things which are done by them in secret. But all things become visible when they are exposed by the light, for everything that becomes visible is light (Eph. 5:8-13).

The key phrases here are "expose them" and "all things become visible when they are exposed by the light." To ignore evil is to encourage it; to keep quiet about it is to help promote it. The Greek verb translated "expose" conveys the idea of reproof, correction, punishment, or discipline.

Sometimes such exposure and reproof will be direct and at other times indirect, but it should always be immediate in the face of anything that is sinful. When we live in obedience to God, that in itself will be a testimony against wrong. When those around us see us helping rather than exploiting, hear us talking with purity instead of profanity, and observe us speaking truthfully rather than deceitfully, our example will itself be a rebuke of selfishness, unwholesome talk, and falsehood. Simply refusing to participate in a dishonest business or social practice will sometimes be such a strong rebuke that it costs us our job or a friendship. Dishonesty is terribly uncomfortable in the presence of honesty, even when there is no verbal or other direct opposition.

Often, of course, open rebuke is necessary. Silent testimony will only go so far. Failure to speak out against and to practically oppose evil things is a failure to obey God. Believers are to expose them in whatever legitimate, biblical ways are necessary.

Unfortunately, many Christians are so barely able to keep their own spiritual and moral houses in order that they do not have the discernment, inclination, or power to confront evil in the church or society at large. That's why it is imperative that we be so mature in biblical truth, and in obedience, holiness, and love, that the natural course of our lives will be to expose, rebuke, and offer remedy for every kind of evil.

Making salvation attractive is a high calling, but we will fail in that endeavor unless we can demonstrate that we have indeed been delivered from sin. Rebuke of sin in others without an accompanying lifestyle of righteousness is the greatest hypocrisy. But lives characterized by purity, power, and joy reflect the order, beauty, and power of a saving God. When we make salvation beautiful, we make God attractive.

To convince a man God can save I need to show him a man He saved. To convince a man that God can give hope I need to show him a man with hope. To convince a man that God can give peace, joy, and love, I need to show him a man with peace, joy, and love. To convince a man that God can give complete, total, and utter satisfaction, I need to show him a satisfied man. When the world sees people who are holy, righteous, peaceful, joyful, and fulfilled, they see the evidence of God's transforming power.

At stake is the eternal destiny of unredeemed souls. Christians who are unholy lead unbelievers to slander God; those who are holy lead them to glorify God. The central issue in holy living is evangelism. A powerful church is not built on its strategy, but on the virtue and holiness of its people. What we believe is linked to how we live and how we live is directly linked to the effectiveness of our Gospel proclamation.

Men and women are different by God's design, and the ultimate purpose for that design displays the beauty and order inherent in God's creation. To do anything less than maintain His order is to bring reproach on His name. If we continue as a church to fall victim to the satanic plotting of the feminist movement, we are permitting Satan to destroy the priority, purity, and integrity of the church. We are allowing him to pull down the Word of God from its lofty position. We are giving our opponents reason to criticize us. And we are helping Satan to blind "the minds of the unbelieving, that they might not see the light of the gospel of the glory of Christ, who is the image of God" (2 Cor. 4:4). That's why it is imperative, for the sake of the kingdom, that you be "blameless and innocent, children of God above reproach in the midst of a crooked and perverse generation, among whom you appear as lights in the world" (Phil. 2:15).

Personal and Group Study Guide

Before beginning your personal or group study of *Different by Design*, take time to read these introductory comments.

If you are working through the study on your own, you may want to adapt certain sections (for example, the icebreakers), and record your responses to all questions in a separate notebook. You might find it more enriching or motivating to study with a partner with whom you can share answers or insights.

If you are leading a group, you may want to ask your group members to read each assigned chapter and work through the study questions before the group meets. This isn't always easy for busy adults, so encourage them with occasional phone calls or notes between meetings. Help members manage their time by suggesting that they identify a regular time of the day or week that they can devote to the study. They too may want to write their responses to the questions in a notebook. *To help keep group discussion focused on the material in* Different by Design, *it is important that each member have his or her own copy of the book.*

Notice that each session includes the following features:

Chapter Theme — a brief statement summarizing the chapter.
Icebreaker — an activity to help each member get better acquainted with the session topic or with each other.
Group Discovery Questions — a list of questions to encourage individual discovery or group participation.
Personal Application Questions — an aid to applying the knowledge gained through study to one's personal living. (Note: These are important questions for group members to answer for themselves, even if they do not wish to discuss their responses in the meeting.)
Focus on Prayer — suggestions for turning one's learning into prayer.

Assignment — activities or preparation to complete prior to the next session.

Here are a few tips that can help you more effectively lead small-group studies:

Pray for each group member, asking the Lord to help you create an open atmosphere where everyone will feel free to talk with one another and with you.

Encourage group members to bring their Bibles as well as their texts to each session. This guide is based on the *New American Standard Bible,* but it is good to have several translations on hand for purposes of comparison.

Start and end on time. This is especially important for the first meeting because it will set the pattern for the rest of the sessions.

Begin with prayer, asking the Holy Spirit to open hearts and minds and to give understanding so that truth will be applied.

Involve everyone. As learners, we retain only 10 percent of what we hear; 20 percent of what we see; 65 percent of what we hear and see; but 90 percent of what we hear, see, and do.

Promote a relaxed environment. Arrange the chairs in a circle or semicircle. This allows eye contact among members and encourages dynamic discussion. Be relaxed in your own attitude and manner. Be willing to share yourself.

Christians have reinterpreted the Bible's teaching on the role of women. Others have reinterpreted the first few chapters of Genesis in a futile attempt to harmonize the biblical account of Creation with the pseudo-science of evolution. Some insist that the Bible doesn't teach all the principles necessary to address life's problems. The faith "once for all delivered to the saints" (Jude 3) has too often become like a weather vane — shifting with each passing wind of change. What is the ultimate source of authority in your life? When faced with a conflict between biblical teaching and a contemporary idea, what do you do? Do you reinterpret the Bible, or reject the idea? Are you willing to take a stand for God's Word? Study Psalm 19:7-11 to see how God describes His Word, and determine to uphold it.

2. Read Matthew 4:1-11. How did Jesus respond when Satan tempted Him? Based on Jesus' pattern, what should Eve have done when Satan tempted her? How do you deal with temptation? Do you follow Eve's or Jesus' pattern? The most effective way to deal with any temptation is to respond biblically. But that presupposes that you know what God's Word teaches. Thus it is imperative that you saturate your mind with God's Word so that you can resist temptation.

Focus on Prayer
Ask God to open your mind to the instruction from His Word that is contained in this book. As you study through the remaining chapters, ask God to reinforce truth you already know and to confirm in your heart truth you were unaware of until now. Ask Him to give you opportunities to apply them.

Assignment
Make a list of those people who exercise some type of authority over you. They may be family members, business associates, or even people you've never met. Then make a list of those people over whom you exercise some type of authority. Next to each name on those lists, write one word that describes the ease or difficulty of the relationship. In other words, does your authority or submission come easily, with moderate difficulty, or is it simply impossible?

2

The Case for Authority and Submission

Chapter Theme: One of the many questions the Apostle Paul faced from the Corinthian church was on the matter of the submission of women. First Corinthians 11:3-16 is Paul's clear statement on the biblical principle of authority and submission.

Icebreakers

1. What are some ways that women manifest independence in our culture? What are some ways men abuse their positions of authority, specifically with regard to women? How much independence for women do you think is justified? Please explain your reasoning.

2. The Apostle Paul cited a culturally relevant example to help explain the principle of authority and submission. If he were alive today and looked to our culture for an example, what might he choose? How would he use that example to teach the principle of authority and submission?

Group Discovery Questions

1. What were conditions like for women in the culture of Paul's day? Why did feminism gain in popularity? (pp. 31–32)

2. Explain the principle of submission. How is it manifested in society? (pp. 32–33)

3. How have evangelical feminists attempted to redefine the meaning of "head" in 1 Corinthians 11:3? (pp. 33–34)

4. Why is a clear understanding of Galatians 3:28 vital to any discussion of the principle of authority and submission? What does that passage teach about men and women? (pp. 34–37)

5. In what way did Christianity elevate women to a position they had not known previously? (p. 37)

6. What are the three manifestations of authority and submission as described by Paul? (1 Cor. 11:3) (p. 38)

7. When and where is it appropriate for women to pray or proclaim God's Word? (pp. 39–40)

8. In the Corinthian church, what was a wife communicating by wearing a head covering? What was a woman revealing by her failure to wear a head covering? (pp. 40–41)

9. In what ways are men and women equal? In what ways are they different? (pp. 43–44)

10. In what ways does nature testify to the differences between men and women? (pp. 44–45)

Personal Application Questions

1. When we examine the principle of authority and submission, it is easy for us to focus in on our human relationships and forget our relationship to Christ. We can't allow Paul's statement that "Christ is the head of every man" to go unnoticed. Since all authority has been given to Jesus in heaven and on earth, what should be your response to His Word? Do you obey all His commands, or only those you find coincide with your desires? Remember, Christ is your Lord and He requires *complete* obedience.

2. How do you respond to people in authority over you who know less than you in their particular sphere of influence? Do you follow their leadership willingly or do you chafe under their authority? Based on what you've learned, what must be your proper response and why?

Focus on Prayer

If you are currently having trouble submitting to someone in authority over you, confess it to God. Ask Him to show you ways in which you can be positive and encouraging to the individual in question. Begin to pray for him or her by realizing that responsibility carries its own burdens.

Assignment

For the next week make a list of the various ways marriages are portrayed in our society, either through advertising, media, or personal experience. Note how many biblical commands or patterns each one violates. Which one comes the closest to God's ideal and why?

3

Marriage As It Was Meant to Be

Chapter Theme: In spite of the curse on marriage because of the Fall, men and women can experience fulfilled marriages in Christ by following the biblical pattern and the example of Christ's love for the church.

Icebreakers

1. In what ways do you think marriage has changed in the last twenty to thirty years? How do you think the society's view of marriage has influenced the outworking of a typical Christian marriage today?

2. How would you characterize the perfect marriage? What should the husband contribute? What should the wife contribute? Even with their contributions, what must be present before the marriage can ever be complete?

Group Discovery Questions

1. Catalog the different ways that the current American family has failed. According to Paul, what contributes to the demise of the family? (pp. 49–51)

2. What is necessary before God's design for marriage will ever be a success? (pp. 52–53)

3. What should characterize a wife's submission to her husband? What should characterize a husband's treatment of his wife? (pp. 53–54)

4. To whom are we really submitting when we submit to those in authority over us? (p. 55)

5. To whom should a husband look when he wants to know how he should treat his wife? (p. 57)

6. What advantage do Christian men have in their love for their wives that unbelieving men don't have? (pp. 57–58)

7. In what ways is God's love different from the world's concept of love? (pp. 57–58)

8. What ought to be the goal of a husband's love for his wife? (p. 60)

9. How should husbands care for their wives? (pp. 61–62)

10. What are some barriers to successful marriages? (p. 64)

Personal Application Questions

1. What is shaping your expectations for marriage: the world's fantasies or God's realities? Sit down with your spouse or fiancé and list the expectations that each of you has for the other. Next, determine which of those have a biblical foundation. In that way you can resolve potential conflicts before they start. Focus on what you can give to your partner rather than what you can get. By doing so, you will help to prevent any expectations from not being met.

2. Men, if you love a woman, you should do everything in your power to preserve her purity. Do you ever encourage her to compromise her spiritual or moral standards? What are you doing to draw her closer to God and to make her life more virtuous? Recognizing your natural concern for your own body and the fact that it is the temple of the Holy Spirit, make sure you care for your wife with at least the same amount of zeal.

Focus on Prayer

With the pressures of the world as great as they are, Christian couples must make Christ the focus of their relationship. As a couple, make sure that you both set aside time together each day to go before the Lord, praying for each other's needs, spiritual as well as physical and emotional. Even when you're not together, make sure you pray for your spouse and for the concerns of that day. You'll find that your relationship will grow deeper and stronger as a result.

Assignment

What are the spiritual, physical, and economic priorities of your family? If you had to eliminate one or more pursuits, what would they be? How much of what you do has a biblical focus? Is anything you are doing clearly forbidden by God's Word? Over the next week think through each of these issues, asking God to give you wisdom regarding any tough decisions you need to make.

4

The Excellent Wife at Work

Chapter Theme: In spite of what society claims, the Bible clearly states that women are to be "workers at home" so that they can fulfill God's design for them and their families.

Icebreakers

1. If you are a worker at home, how would you answer those who claim you are hindering your potential by not pursuing a career or some job outside the home?

2. Economic hardship faces many Christian couples who are committed to the biblical pattern for the family. What are some avenues you might pursue that could bring in extra income yet allow the wife to be a "worker at home"?

Group Discussion Questions

1. What events helped create an environment in the United States conducive to the growth of the traditional family? (p. 68)

2. What factors led to the fall of the traditional family of the '50s? (p. 69)

3. What was expected of wives in the first century? (p. 71)

4. Explain why a woman's responsibility is the home (pp. 72–73).

5. Name some of the problems families face when the wife goes to work outside the home (p. 73).

6. What ought to be the overriding concern in any plans for the wife to work outside the home? (p. 75)

7. What characteristics should men look for in a wife? (p. 76)

8. Describe the selfless love of the Proverbs 31 woman for her husband (pp. 76–77).

9. What types of business abilities must a wife combine if she desires to pattern her life after the Proverbs 31 woman? (p. 78)

10. What activities of the Proverbs 31 woman reveal her motivation and self-discipline? (pp. 78–79)

11. What was the legacy of the Proverbs 31 woman? (p. 81)

Personal Application Questions

1. If you are a mother who works outside the home, analyze why you are working. By the time you deduct taxes, child care costs, clothing, and transportation expenses, how much extra income are you actually providing? Set aside time with your husband to honestly evaluate your present circumstances. Are there some sacrifices you both could make or some other means by which you could remain at home yet contribute to the financial needs of your family?

2. If you are a mother who is staying at home with your children, are you taking advantage of your opportunity to shape their lives for godly living? Or is your time spent unproductively with television programs that might be tearing down the very principles you are trying to instill into your family's life? Make sure every day has spiritual input so that your children begin looking at life from God's perspective. Prepare them for society's secular influence by teaching godly values (Prov. 22:6; 2 Tim. 3:15).

Focus on Prayer

Anything you decide to do regarding your family's financial picture ought to be bathed in prayer. Ask God to clarify in your heart the wisdom from His Word regarding this topic. Allow Him to guide you in these vital decisions. But be sure you are willing to make sacrifices if He leads you in that direction.

Assignment

Meditate as a family on Colossians 3:12-21, using those verses as a guideline for a devotional time together. Determine what qualities mentioned in the passage are lacking or weak in your family. Confess to one another the wrong attitudes and actions each has been exhibiting. After you choose an area you need to concentrate on, pray for one another that each may be strengthened to live the quality of life that glorifies Christ.

5

A Different Place in God's Plan

Chapter Theme: God's ideal for marriage is foreign to many people in the church. But God has left us with encouragement and instruction from His Word.

Icebreakers
1. Christians who are married to unbelievers face a difficult life that few of us can relate to. If you are married to an unbeliever, how do you live out your faith? If you know someone who is in that situation, what do you do to offer encouragement?
2. Widows, divorcees, and single people are often ignored in many churches. If you are one of that number, how do you handle that kind of treatment? Do you secretly wish that you had a different marital status? Why?

Group Discovery Questions
1. What does Paul counsel a Christian not to do if he or she is married to an unbeliever? (pp. 84–85)
2. How can a believer sanctify a home? (pp. 84–85)
3. What are some things that a Christian wife can do that could help lead her unbelieving husband to Christ? (pp. 86–88)
4. What are some things that a Christian husband can do that could lead his unbelieving wife to embrace Christ? (pp. 88–90)
5. Who would qualify as a widow in the biblical sense? (p. 90)
6. How can the church decide which widows should receive financial support? (pp. 92–94)
7. Who has the primary responsibility for caring for widows? (p. 92)
8. What qualities ought to characterize those widows who wish to serve the church in an official capacity? (pp. 94–96)
9. How should the church encourage younger widows? (pp. 94–96)

10. Describe the gift of singleness as Paul explains it (p. 100).
11. What can single people do to control their desires if they do not have the gift of singleness? (pp. 101–2)
12. What are some of the advantages of being single? (pp. 102–5)

Personal Application Questions

1. The wife is to be submissive, faithful, and modest toward her husband; and the husband is to show consideration, chivalry, and companionship toward his wife. Answer the following practical questions as a way of measuring those virtues in your life:

- Are you faithful to maintain your spiritual life through Bible study, prayer, regular church attendance, and fellowship with God's people?
- Do you ask forgiveness when you have done something wrong?
- Do you accept corrective criticisms graciously?
- Do you make excessive demands on your mate, expecting too much from him or her?
- Do you allow your spouse to make mistakes without condemning him or her?
- Do you focus on what you appreciate about your mate, or do you tend to find fault with him or her?
- When you disagree with your mate, do you seek biblical answers for the problem instead of blowing up emotionally or verbally attacking your mate?
- Are you a good listener when your mate tries to explain something?

If you've spotted some problems in your life, prayerfully seek to make the necessary corrections. To help you in your resolve, seek the counsel and accountability of a godly friend who is a fellow wife or husband.

2. Does your church have a ministry to widows? Is it fulfilling its biblical responsibility to care for the godly women in its midst who have no means of support? If not, would you be instrumental in praying with your pastor about such a ministry and helping to initiate it? As a preventative measure

against the church's being overburdened, consider having a financial planner or tax adviser give a seminar to your church members on how they can prepare for the premature death of a breadwinner and for their retirement years.

3. The Apostle Paul was convinced that, because of conflict with the world system, single believers should seriously consider the possibility of remaining as they are. Are you presently struggling with your singleness? If you are, would you seriously consider Paul's advice? Ask God to confirm in your heart whether He would rather you be single or married.

Focus on Prayer
Prayerfully consider the verses below and allow God to give you an awareness of others' needs and an increasing desire to help them:

- Romans 13:8—"Owe nothing to anyone except to love one another; for he who loves his neighbor has fulfilled the law."
- Galatians 5:14—"The whole Law is fulfilled in ... the statement, 'You shall love your neighbor as yourself.' "
- 1 John 3:11, 16-17—"For this is the message which you have heard from the beginning, that we should love one another.... We know love by this, that He laid down His life for us; and we ought to lay down our lives for the brethren. But whoever has the world's goods, and beholds his brother in need and closes his heart against him, how does the love of God abide in him?"

Assignment
True religion involves visiting "widows in their distress" (James 1:27). Visiting speaks of caring for needy women and their children, and distress refers to anything that burdens or pressures the spirit. Practical deeds of love can help relieve their pressures and burdens. Helping them around the house or taking them with you on trips are simple but important ways to uplift them. Create a list of ways you can serve. Then begin to do the actions on your list.

6

The Church's Leading Men

Chapter Theme: While women have unique opportunities for service in the church, God has specifically called men to provide the authority and leadership of the church.

Icebreakers
1. Suppose you went to a Bible study with both men and women and found that a woman regularly led the prayer time. How would you respond? What opinion could that lead you to form regarding the leadership of the Bible study?
2. Have you ever had any disagreement with anyone in leadership in your church? If so, how did the leader respond to you? How was the disagreement ultimately resolved? What positive or negative impressions did that situation leave you with?

Group Discovery Questions
1. Who has the unique responsibility of offering public prayer on behalf of the lost? (p. 111)
2. With what are we to offer our prayers? (p. 112)
3. Why is the character of a leader more important than his aptitude? (p. 114)
4. What is the fundamental, universal requirement of all God's leaders? Why is it so important? (p. 115)
5. Explain the phrase "husband of one wife." Why is this a significant qualification for a church leader? (p. 116)
6. Why is sobriety included in the list of qualifications for a church leader? (pp. 116–17, 120)
7. What are the criteria that set apart a man who is skilled in teaching God's Word? (p. 120)
8. How can the love of money corrupt a man's ministry? (p. 121)
9. Where should a church leader first demonstrate his spiritual leadership? Why? (pp. 122–23)
10. Why does Paul warn against putting a new convert into a leadership position? (p. 123)

11. How should a church leader be viewed by the unbelieving community? (p. 124)

Personal Application Questions

1. Church leadership is a sacred task requiring the highest level of spiritual credibility and maturity. Sadly, some people pursue it for the wrong reasons, such as for money, job security, or prestige. If you are in a position of spiritual leadership, what are your motives? Read 1 Peter 5:2-4. What is the compelling motive for anyone to pursue leadership in God's house? Be sure that you guard your motives carefully.

2. Credibility is the key to effective teaching—your life must model your lesson. That's true even if you aren't a preacher or teacher in the formal sense. We are all teaching something to those who watch us, and they often learn more from our actions than from our words. What are you teaching those who observe your life? Are they learning holiness or hypocrisy?

Focus on Prayer

Cultivating a disciplined mind requires that you constantly expose it to what is good. What things do you meditate on? Should some of those things be eliminated? If so, ask God to help you be more disciplined in your thinking as you learn to focus on what is true, honorable, right, pure, lovely, of good repute, excellent, and worthy of praise.

Assignment

Perhaps you've been wondering if you have been called into the ministry. If so, now is the time to honestly evaluate your life against the biblical qualifications. After you finish your evaluation, ask your pastor or other leaders in your church to evaluate you as well. They may confirm or question your readiness for such a role. Whatever their response, ask them to continue to encourage you, guide your training, and hold you accountable.

7

God's High Call for Women

Chapter Theme: Two passages in Scripture, 1 Timothy 2:11-15 and 1 Corinthians 14:33-35, are the authoritative word on the limitations of women's roles in the church. They are not the Apostle Paul's attempt to confine women to a second-class status; they are an affirmation of God's perfect design.

Icebreakers
1. How would you characterize the way you dress when you attend church: conservative, contemporary, liberal, or ostentatious? Would others characterize your dress in the same way or differently? What kind of dress do you think honors God the most?
2. If you are a woman, do you think God has blessed you with the gift of teaching or leadership? If so, how are you using those gifts? Does your teaching or leadership involve exercising authority over men in some ministry of the church? How do you reconcile that with 1 Timothy 2:11-15 and 1 Corinthians 14:33-35?

Group Discovery Questions
1. How do some people try to disprove the trustworthiness of 1 Timothy 2:9-15 and 1 Corinthians 14:33-35? (pp. 127–29)
2. Why is the wearing of expensive, elaborate clothes and jewelry inappropriate for women in the church? What should they wear instead? (pp. 131–32)
3. What ought to characterize a woman's approach to worship? (pp. 132–33)
4. According to 1 Timothy 2:11, what role are women to have during the worship service? How did Paul's instruction differ from the accepted practice for those who came from a Jewish background? (pp. 134–35)
5. According to the Old Testament, in what ways were women equal to men? What roles did they not share with men? (pp. 135–36)

6. How does the New Testament support the teaching of the Old Testament regarding women's roles? (pp. 136–37)

7. What one word best characterizes the role of a woman as a learner? Explain (pp. 137–38).

8. What exactly does Paul forbid women from doing in the context of the worship service or any ministry involving men? (pp. 138–39)

9. What similar instruction did Paul give the Corinthians? (1 Cor. 14:33-35, pp. 139–40)

10. What are some appropriate circumstances when women can proclaim God's truth? (pp. 140–41)

11. In what way does Paul use the circumstances that occurred at the Fall to corroborate the differing roles for men and women that God established in the order of creation? (pp. 141–42)

12. What is a woman's greatest opportunity for influencing society? Explain (pp. 143–44).

13. What are some ways that women can use their spiritual gifts yet still fulfill the teaching of 1 Timothy 2:11-15? (pp. 144–45)

Personal Application Questions

1. What did Paul mean when he said that women were to keep silent in the church? Did this simply refer to the Corinthian women in the Corinthian church? Explain. How does this apply to the trend today of women in the pulpit? Should a woman who is mature spiritually and gifted in teaching take over the preaching in a church where there isn't a man available to do the job? How should women who are gifted in teaching exercise their gifts?

2. Some women in the Ephesian and Corinthian churches were more concerned with their rights than their responsibilities to God and the church. What about you? Is your focus on getting or giving? Do you more frequently demand your rights or fulfill your responsibilities? Remember that Jesus came not "to be served, but to serve" (Matt. 20:28). If your focus has gradually changed from ministering to the needs of others to looking out for your own rights, you can help get it back where it belongs by memorizing Philippians 2:3-4.

Focus on Prayer

The church at Ephesus had been influenced by the prevailing views of society regarding women. The same could be said about the church today. In this as in other areas, the church has been influenced by the world instead of being an influence on the world. Are your views of current issues being shaped by the prevailing opinions of society, or by God's Word? Perhaps you need to rethink your position on such issues as women's roles, abortion, homosexuality, creation and evolution, the Christian's responsibility to government, lawsuits, and divorce and remarriage. Spend some time in prayer and ask God to give you the courage to take a stand on the issues based on His Word—no matter what society propagates. Then pray that the church as a whole will also stand firm for God's truth.

Assignment

Women can (under the right circumstances) proclaim God's truth. Do you regularly look for opportunities to share the truths of Scripture with your friends? your neighbors? your spouse? your children? To share the truths of the Bible we must first learn them ourselves. That requires constant study. If you aren't regularly studying Scripture, make a commitment to the Lord to begin tomorrow.

8

The Character of Service

Chapter Theme: While not many men are cut out for leadership in the church, it is the duty of all believers to serve the body of Christ. They can do so in both official and unofficial ways. First Timothy 3:8-13 and Titus 2:1-8 delineate the characteristics that ought to exemplify all believers willing to serve.

Icebreakers

1. What thoughts and perceptions do you usually associate with the word "deacon"? Do you view a deacon more as a leader or as a servant? Why?

2. What do you suppose is a good age to stop ministering to others? At what age should you begin serving others? What have you learned from older believers? What have you learned from younger Christians?

Group Discovery Questions

1. What happens to the church when individual believers don't serve with the unique abilities God gave them? (pp. 147–48)

2. What are the three levels of service the Bible delineates? (pp. 148–49)

3. In what way do deacons specifically assist the elders? (p. 149)

4. What qualities ought to be true of a deacon's personal character? Explain each one (pp. 150–52).

5. Out of necessity, what is the foundation of a deacon's spiritual character? (p. 152)

6. What overarching quality that is to be true of elders must also characterize deacons? Why? (p. 153)

7. What factors indicate that Paul established a separate office for women deacons? (p. 154)

8. What rewards await those who serve well as deacons? (p. 155)

9. What characteristics and virtues should be manifested by older men in the church? In what way does their experience

194 Different by Design

of years heighten those qualities? (pp. 156–58)

10. What are older women in the church to be busy doing? Why is this such a vital ministry? (pp. 159–60)

11. What are the older women to teach the younger women to do? (Titus 2:4-5) Explain each one (pp. 160–62).

12. What kind of dangers do young Christian men face in our society? (pp. 162–63)

13. What godly qualities should young men cultivate? (pp. 164–65)

Personal Application Questions

1. Review the personal character qualifications of a deacon. How would you rate yourself in each of those areas? What kind of changes would you need to make to be known as righteous in those areas? Do some serious self-examination. As you do, realize that the outcome of your examination holds greater significance than merely the possibility of a future role as a deacon. It means you will have a greater capacity for glorifying God.

2. To what degree are you actively using your gifts in serving the church? If you are an older believer, are you investing your life in someone who can gain practical wisdom from your experience? If you are a younger believer, are you allowing yourself to be held accountable to someone older so that you can arm yourself against the temptations of youth?

Focus on Prayer

Perhaps you've been unsure about whether you should pursue a ministry opportunity that has come your way. Or you may be looking for a ministry to serve in. If you haven't already, begin seeking God's guidance. Ask Him to clearly show you where you might serve. Sometimes the best place to start is where you know there are needs. You may find that, as you begin serving in needy places, you have found the very spot where God wants you.

Assignment

According to Acts 6:3, the people were to look for men who were "of good reputation, full of the Spirit and of wisdom."

Acts 6:5 mentions that Stephen was "full of faith." Those characteristics identified seven men of integrity. Can you be characterized as a person of integrity? On a scale of 1–10, how would you rate yourself in each of those four characteristics? In which one are you the weakest? Make it your goal this week to improve your Christian walk in that area. For example, if you are weakest in your faith, look up "faith" in a concordance and do a word study on that topic. Or, you might make a list of all the times God has been faithful in blessing your life; in turn, that will increase your faith in Him.

9

For the Sake of the Kingdom

Chapter Theme: Holy, righteous lives are the backbone of the Gospel we proclaim. That's why it is critical that Christians live in such a way that will cause unbelievers to investigate the claims of Christianity.

Icebreaker
What have you found to be your most effective means of evangelism? Do you find it easier to talk about Christ to someone you don't know or to a friend or relative? What do you think those unbelievers who are closest say about you when you're not around?

Group Discovery Questions
1. Why does God want His people to live holy lives? (p. 167)
2. In what ways can we bring dishonor on God's Word? (p. 169)
3. Why don't unbelievers want to be confronted by people whose lives are transformed by Christ? (p. 170)
4. What ought to be our primary message to our world about God? Why? (p. 171)
5. Before unbelievers can be attracted to the Gospel, what must they come to realize about their own lives? (pp. 171–72)
6. What are we ultimately doing if we allow Satan a free reign to push his feminist agenda within the church? (pp. 173)

Practical Application Question
Before Jesus ascended into heaven, He commanded His disciples to "Go . . . make disciples of all nations" (Matt. 28:19). In so doing He established evangelism as the number one priority for the church. But many Christians act as if the responsibility for evangelism belongs to the pastor or the church evangelism committee. What about you? Are you concerned about the lost? When was the last time you spoke to an unbeliever about Christ? Are you currently praying for someone's salvation? Cultivate relationships with unbeliev-

ers, and take every opportunity to speak to them about the Lord.

Focus on Prayer

If evangelism has been difficult for you, ask God to give you a love for the lost. If you aren't already doing so, begin praying for someone's salvation. Ask God to give you opportunities to present the Gospel. And ask Him to help you lead the kind of life that will make unbelievers curious about Christ.

Assignment

The goal of this book has been to give you a clearer picture of God's will, both general and specific, for your life. What new insights have you gained? What new truths have you learned? Now you need to begin to apply them to your life. Also, when you have the opportunity, be sure you uphold God's Word in the midst of the perverse society in which we live.

1
Creation to Corruption

Chapter Theme: God's perfect design for men and women, which He established at creation, includes their functional differences. All of this became corrupted by sin and Satan. Although through Christ men and women can live according to God's design, Satan tries to corrupt Christ's work both in marriage and the church.

Icebreakers *(Choose one)*
1. List several ways in which you have seen personally the influence of the feminist movement in your church. How have they altered the biblical pattern for men's and women's roles?
2. The first sin details the reversal of male/female roles. If you are a woman, relate an incident where you usurped a man's leadership position. If you are a man, describe a time when you allowed a woman to usurp a specific leadership role you held. What were the consequences?

Group Discovery Questions
1. What kind of damage has the feminist movement caused for both society and the church? (pp. 15–16)
2. In what ways did Adam and Eve have a perfect relationship before sin entered the world? (pp. 18–20)
3. Describe the specific sins Adam and Eve committed at the Fall (p. 21).
4. In what ways does the curse affect the most basic elements of life? (pp. 21–22)
5. What part of society does Satan specifically attack? Why? (p. 24)
6. In what ways does Gnosticism convolute the biblical creation account? (pp. 25–26)
7. What is the goal of New Age theology? (p. 27)

Personal Application Questions
1. Christians today tend to compromise biblical teaching and standards. Under pressure from the feminist movement, some

SCRIPTURE INDEX

200

SUBJECT INDEX